the AMBITIOUS WOMAN

What It Takes and Why You Want To Be One

ESTHER SPINA

Motivational Press®
LEADERS IN GLOBAL PUBLISHING

Published by Motivational Press, Inc.
1777 Aurora Road
Melbourne, Florida, 32935
www.MotivationalPress.com

Manufactured in the United States of America.

ISBN: 978-1-62865-522-3

Contents

Dedication

This book is dedicated to the "Ambitious Women" in my family, and those who are yet to come.

My daughter Rachel; you are just beginning to live your full potential. I love you *so* much, I can't stop loving you!

My two daughters-in-love, Amanda and Leah; you are the daughters of "my heart." God has twice blessed me with both of you.

My 3 granddaughters, Kate, Esther, Hannah, I pray you will grow up to believe that with God's help, you can be or do *anything* you desire.

Finally to my granddaughters who may be born in the future; may you fulfill the dreams and destiny that God already has planned for you, plans that he created even before you were born.

Foreword

I've known Esther for all my life. I'm her younger sister, born 13 months after her. And I can tell you this: The book you are about to read is not all about her. Yes, you will read about her life, about how each of the chapters has impacted her to make her the Ambitious Woman she is today. But the book is truly about you. Knowing Esther's heart as I do, she wants to connect with you—heart to heart.

Esther believes in serendipity, meaning "a combination of events that are not individually beneficial, but occurring together to produce a good or wonderful outcome." But she also believes that God authors all events in our lives. Even though she has never met you, this book is her serendipitous moment in time to reach you, to help you, to come alongside you to be the woman—the Ambitious Woman—that you've always wanted to be.

In my mind, Esther is the perfect example of ambition. She models each of the characteristics presented in the chapters you are about to read. As you read each chapter, you'll understand what it means to be an Ambitious Woman. People have been encouraging Esther to write this book for years. She has such vision; she's goal- oriented and purpose-driven. She leaves nothing to "chance" but thinks things through, then acts.

Finally, when she had the confirmation she should be writing a book, she realized it could not be solely about herself; she had met too many others who had poured into her life in very significant ways. Some are famous women whom she only knows from afar, while others are close and important to her daily life. This book includes stories about some of these people—people she believes can affect your life in positive and meaningful ways.

There is something else I'd like to share with you about Esther. Esther is a woman of great faith. She believes in the God of the Bible, and her faith will be evident as you read through the elements of ambition together. Why is this important? Because what you believe in is foundational to any Ambitious Woman.

The Beginnings of this Book

In late 2013, Esther began to feel that the time had finally come to share her Ambitious Woman Journey. It was time to apply what she had learned and compile it into a book for all women to read. The ministry she is starting, her life, and this book are *"for such a time as this,"* a term she has used from one of her favorite books in the Bible, the Book of Esther. Where else?

When Esther and I started talking about this book, she told me, "I want to inspire women to their greatness. God has allowed me to go through many things so that I could reach women on different levels of life. I want women everywhere to know that they are amazing; they are powerful; they can do what they put their minds to because they are ambitious. For some, it is a matter of that ambition being drawn out. For others, it is time for their ambition to be 'let loose' in their lives. And for women everywhere, this is your time to do what you were created to do!"

Esther's life and her words have inspired me to be ambitious and to accomplish things I never thought were possible. My prayer for you is that, as you read, you'll be inspired to do what you were created to do.

So I congratulate you, in advance, for becoming the Ambitious Woman you were meant to be. May the journey you start today never end!

Sincerely,

Elizabeth "Betsy" Cline

Introduction

When you hear the word *ambitious*, what comes to mind? Power-hungry? Getting ahead no matter what it takes? Someone who runs over others to accomplish her goals?

I think that many people have a negative view of what it means to be ambitious. However, the real definition of ambition is "having or showing a strong desire and determination to succeed." You may be ambitious to succeed in business. To be the best mom you can be. To have a successful ministry. Or to be the best person you can possibly be.

I see ambition in people who inspire others, who empower and motivate them to accomplish their goals. Ambitious people are humble and loyal; they are disciplined and have a never-give-up attitude.

Why do I see these traits? While some ambitious people are "all about me," I have had the privilege of meeting countless others who truly do care about people. They are "ambitious" about seeing others succeed. They are ambitious … and I am too.

Life has a way of humbling all of us. I've learned to be ambitious in a positive way because of the rocky roads I've had to travel. In the pages you are about to read, I will tell you of my experiences, good and not so good, as well as those of others, famous and not-so-famous, who have learned to be ambitious in ways that will encourage and instill passion in you.

I believe you are an Ambitious Woman. Why do I say that? Because you are about to read this book.

Now you may be thinking, "I'm not ambitious. I don't have 'what it takes.' I feel alone, empty, and don't know what I'm doing much of the time." Here's a truth: Most people are not born ambitious; it's a choice they make. It's a mindset. A determination. No one can make you ambitious, but when you decide to become this way, you will find that your life changes—radically.

Becoming ambitious is a choice you make as you grow in life, in your career, or at home. You choose to be ambitious; in doing so, you can become successful in whatever is important to you. Once you decide, you can then take the steps necessary that will lead to your success.

Desire alone is not enough. You have to take *action*. In fact, you have to take *massive action*. I want to show you how to choose to be ambitious and to take massive action.

Ambition always follows choice. What do you have to choose? You must choose to do the things that unsuccessful people won't do. They refuse to move beyond their own woe-is-me mindset. They see obstacles to their goals and give up. They let fear stop them before they even start. They allow what others tell them to dictate what they will and won't do.

But you are not that person.

I've found in my business that "people want to do what I do," but they "don't want to do what I do." Does that make sense? If you want to be successful, then you must choose to do what ambitious people do. How about the stay-at-home mom who knows how to handle her kids and keeps her home running smoothly—she's successful. What about the woman who can balance her career and a family—she's successful. The woman who is determined to earn her degree, the woman who is a visionary and is making her dream a reality, the woman who is consistent in character and in the way she lives life—they are all successful. Why? Because they are Ambitious Women.

Being ambitious will lead to success, no doubt, but to be ambitious you must develop the traits and characteristics of an Ambitious Woman. That is what I will show you in the following pages: what you need to do to be an Ambitious Woman. And I have learned all of this not from being born with each trait and characteristic, but from developing and experiencing them throughout my life.

A Little About Me

My most successful business endeavors have come through commission-only sales. When I first started in sales almost twenty years ago, I had experience in traditional business, but in the sales business, I had to start at the bottom and learn the ropes. That meant I needed to be humble and do a lot of things I did *not* want to do. I learned what works and what doesn't by following those who were successful. I was willing to do what others didn't/wouldn't/chose not to do.

When I got into "direct" sales years ago, I followed the path laid out by the company and its founders and stayed true to it. Trust me; that was hard. I like doing things my way, and the path humbled me. But I became successful because I chose to be humble, and it helped me be more ambitious from the onset.

Ambition will come to you as well. However, you cannot wait until you "feel" ambitious. You must decide what you want to do, what you want to change about yourself, or what goal you want to accomplish. Ambition will then begin to be part of your very being as you take your first steps.

I never thought about writing a book; it was never a goal of mine. I thought, *I don't really have an exciting enough life to write about something people would want to read.* So how did I write this book? A few years ago, out of the clear blue sky (I don't even remember what we were talking about), the co- founder of the company I work with looked at me and said, "You're going to write a book someday."

I replied, "What? Me? I don't have anything to say." I truly believed that. But he planted the first seed. He said, "You have a lot of stories to share."

That was the end of that conversation. In the following months and years, as I grew and developed success as an Ambitious Woman, I began to wonder if I should share some of my experiences, share some encouragement and hope with women who desire more in life, and not just keep it all to myself. But I didn't take any steps to make it happen.

In the fall of 2013, I met with a mentor and coach (more about that later in Chapter 15). She encouraged me to begin to leave my legacy and not to be selfish but to share what I have learned with others. One way to leave a legacy is to write a book—not for just a few to read, but hundreds, even thousands of women everywhere. It was exciting! I thought, *Okay I will do it someday*. But God has a way of putting things right in your path, if you're willing to do what you are supposed to be doing.

In January 2014, I was at a Women's Profitability Seminar that I really did not want to attend. I was too busy and getting ready to go out of town. But I pushed through with support for my good friend, Judy Hoberman, who was hosting the event. (You have to read our book, *Pure Wealth: 26 Ways to Crazy Profitability*!)

*****

There is nothing you cannot do with a little ambition, and ambition will come when you make a choice. Ambition is not just about being successful and getting things done. *Ambition is about being determined enough to overcome adversity*. If you want to overcome obstacles in your life, then you will need a determined, ambitious mindset. You must choose to push forward, to be motivated, committed, and purposeful.

I have a motto I've lived by throughout my business career. I have learned to "discipline my disappointments."

When things or people disappoint me, I have my little pity party, then immediately do something constructive to overcome or "discipline my disappointment." During sad and even devastating times, such as losing a child or filing bankruptcy during a recession—both of which I've gone through—I had to come to the point where I decided I was going to be ambitious and successful, no matter what life brought my way. I didn't make it through my trials by being depressed, complacent, or defeated. I made it through by being ambitious.

You can too! You can get through whatever you are facing, and you can accomplish your dreams and goals by choosing to be ambitious. You can encourage yourself to "keep going," even when life is dragging you down.

In my business, there is nothing like a sale, a new recruit, or a new customer to make me forget about my disappointment over that "hot" prospect who just changed his mind. That is how I "discipline my disappointment," and you can do the same thing in your own way. You do something. You take action to move past and move on. That is the most important thing you can do—decide to move on!

Becoming an Ambitious Woman

Without this "ambitious quality" inside of you, I don't believe you can be successful in your endeavor, nor will you become the best person that you can possibly be. You might be asking, "How do I obtain this ambitious quality if I am not born with it?" I'm glad you asked! Here are three things I've learned. If you make these a part of your life, then you will be well on your way to becoming an Ambitious Woman.

Read and develop yourself. Ambition comes through reading books by those who are successful in the area you have chosen and by finding self- development books that help you develop character and integrity. I am sure you have been told this before, but it is true: Ambitious and successful people read all the time. They also attend seminars, conferences, and small groups where they learn and receive encouragement and motivation. They are willing to pay the price. They are willing to **invest** in themselves and not be stingy with their personal development and training. Most people are not willing to invest their own time or money. They think it is not really important enough to spend the money on themselves, or they believe they do not "deserve it." Neither one of these is true. In my opinion, it is the MOST important thing to do, if you truly want to be successful. Ambitious people desire truth and are willing to embrace it, no matter what it shows them about themselves. They act upon that truth by walking down a road of continual improvement. No one ever "arrives." As much as I have been blessed with success, I am always finding inspiring, motivational, and encouraging books to read, seminars to attend, and people with whom to connect.

Here is a truth: If you are not moving forward, you are going backwards. And books are a great way to get you going in the right direction. The first book that helped me move forward was *Beach Money* by Jordan Adler. It was so real and down to earth, and it gave me hope that no matter how many times I fail, if I keep trying I will eventually succeed! I could so relate to Jordan's words, especially because he talked about beach and money, two of my favorite things! Reading books can change your life, and I encourage you do so every day. If you don't know of any good books that pertain to your endeavor, ask those whom you know are succeeding which ones they read.

Be Accountable. I'll talk more on this later, but this is one of the hardest things to do because once you commit you are accountable. When I decided to be successful in direct selling, the first thing I did was to approach the CEO of the company I work with and say, "You don't know me, but I'm going to be someone in this business." He looked at me and smiled. But I didn't do that for him—I did it for *me*. I needed to be accountable, and who better to choose than the CEO and founder? Those words have motivated me to be ambitious. I had committed, and I was not going to back down.

Set goals. Wow, how cliché is that! But honestly it is the key. You have to set goals. There is no way around this; if you want to be ambitious, you have to set ambitious goals, aggressive goals. And if you don't accomplish what you set out to do, don't give up. That's what most people do; they get disappointed and quit. But ambitious people simply reset their goals. That is okay. Nothing is over until *you decide* it's over. You decide how best to reset the path you are on and what changes you need to make to accomplish your goals. That is what ambitious and successful people do. They don't allow negativity or failure to keep them down. Instead, they *choose* to move forward. They keep reaching for their goals until the eleventh hour. Why? Because no one knows what is going to happen tomorrow, next week, or next year.

One of the things I love to do is to watch nonfiction movies and documentaries about people. I also love to read stories, especially true stories, about real people who have become successful. I love how they have pushed through adversity. One thing I find out about all of these people is they are ambitious! So in this book, I have included profiles from some of the people I most admire and respect. Some are famous people for whom I have great admiration and from whose lives I have learned much. Some are people I will never meet, but their stories are amazing! Others are people I know and love dearly; people I would go to the ends of the earth to help, if needed. I hope all of these people inspire you to be the most Ambitious Woman you can be!

Before We Begin

Before we begin looking at what it takes to be an Ambitious Woman, I'd like to leave you with an important thought. Too many people coast through life, letting life happen to them without giving thought to what lies ahead or where they are going. *Esquire* magazine writer and New York socialite Helen Lawrenson once said, "If a woman is sufficiently ambitious, determined, and gifted, there is practically nothing she can't do." It is so important to have direction, to choose a life of ambition, purpose, and intentional growth.

I don't know if you are the type of person who takes notes or keeps a journal. But I am going to suggest something that I do every time I read a book. Take out a highlighter and get a notebook or a journal. As you go through each chapter, highlight all the things you want to reread, remember, and refer to later. Then as you go along, write in your journal some of the suggestions and exercises I have for you. Write down inspirational quotes and recommendations of books mentioned. Write down your thoughts as you read and contemplate what it takes to be an Ambitious Woman and why you want to be one. If you do this, reading the book will bring so much more value.

As you read this book ask yourself, "What could I accomplish if I put forth my best effort? What could I succeed at if I truly and intentionally committed myself to be all that I can be?" What would happen if I really became ambitious … even *radically ambitious*?

Remember, the traits in that ONE word, *Ambitious*, can be all you need to be successful at whatever you attempt.

Now turn to the first chapter, and allow me to help you accomplish your goals and become the Ambitious Woman you were meant to be!

Love and Prayers,

Esther

Chapter 1

Live an Inspired Life

It's Never Too Late

Diana Nyad [1]

Think back to when you were a child. What excited and inspired you? What dreams did you have? What goals did you want to accomplish? What got your juices flowing and had you jumping out of bed in the morning?

What about now? Have you settled for something less than your dreams? Do you think it's too late?

Don't say that to Diana Nyad, broadcast journalist, writer, and record-breaking swimmer.

On Labor Day, September 2, 2013—at the age of 64—Nyad achieved her dream of swimming 110 miles between

1 http://usa.greekreporter.com/files/2013/09/Diana_Nyad_record_swimmer_Greek.jpg

Havana and Key West. In the water for more than two days and continually encouraged by her support team, she became the first person to swim from Cuba to Florida without a shark cage. It was her fifth attempt.

In her own words she says, "I have three messages: One is we should never, ever give up. Two is you never are too old to chase your dreams. Three is it looks like a solitary sport, but it takes a team."

*****

As we begin the chapter together, let's take Nyad's words as our inspiration for beginning our quest to become Ambitious Women. Diana Nyad is an Ambitious Woman! She inspires me by demonstrating that it is not too late to accomplish my goals.

If I can paraphrase, Nyad's message means:

* Never give up.

* It's never too late.

* Build a team to build a dream.

*****

When we first moved to Texas, my husband Frank and I bought a new home. It was a big family house with a double lot yard and large pool, just perfect for raising four children. But after 15 years, the kids were finally on their own and we thought it was time to get a new home – and not just for raising kids! However, we had not updated any part of the house in all the years we had lived in it. We had become comfortable in our environment. We still had popcorn ceilings, gold fixtures, flowered wallpaper, and mauve paint on some of the walls, and green carpet throughout the entire house. As a potential homebuyer, I asked myself, "Would you buy our house?"

The answer was painfully clear.

I wouldn't buy my house, and I was sure no one else would want to either.

The problem was that we wanted to sell the house but we didn't want to lose money doing it. The thought of selling and potentially making money *inspired* me. For the next 24 months, we remodeled each and every room. My inspiration created imagination, which led to creativeness, and my creativity became reality as each room was transformed.

The result? When the house was ready to put on the market, it was a house we could love. In fact, we loved the remodeled home so much, we decided NOT to sell it! For the next two years, we enjoyed the fruit of our labor. Since then, we have found the house of our dreams and moved, and our number two son and his family are enjoying the home we were inspired to transform.

What does this have to do with Diane Nyad?

Well, we could have decided it was too much work, time and money to take on the task of remodeling. Or we could have given up after doing one or two rooms. Or we could have tried to have done every single thing ourselves. (Frank did change more than 50 gold door knobs, however!) Had we not been inspired by our dream of redoing the house, we might never have found the house we live in today.

Did this take us out of our comfort zone? You bet it did. Whatever inspires you will take you out of your comfort zone. Why? Because the things we do well are in our COMFORT ZONES. They've brought us success in the past, and they make us feel good. But there is the catch. The more we stay in our comfort zones, the less growth we experience.

It's just like our house. We were comfortable with green carpet and flowered wallpaper. In order to update the house, we had to get uncomfortable.

Your source of inspiration will drive you to move beyond the status quo. To keep improving. To continually set goals and achieve them. Yes, you may miss the mark sometimes, but inspiration will help you to learn lessons and to accept the fact that life's experiences are built on the mistakes we make—and what we learn from them.

My Inspirations

What does inspiration look like in my life? For the readers who do not know me, I'm a successful businesswoman and the founder of the Ambitious Women Conferences. Here's my story about getting inspired.

In 2006, my husband and I were at a crossroads. He wanted to retire from the construction business; however, the problem was we didn't have any retirement money. We had always owned our own business and been through good times and bad times. The previous 15 years were spent catching up and starting over from the hard-hit recession in the 90s. We knew we had to make a change, especially if I wanted to buy shoes.

You see, I love shoes. All kinds! Flats, high heels, pumps, stilettos, open-toed, sandals, slip-ons, ones with straps … you name them, I love them. I realized I may not always be able to continue buying shoes! And clothes from Boston Proper and White House Black Market … now don't get me started …

I was so inspired, I said "yes" to a new business opportunity. And as I mentioned to you in my introduction, I then introduced myself to the CEO and said, "You don't know me, but I'm going to be somebody in this company someday." He smiled and nodded, as if to say, "Well, let's see if that's true." My interpretation of his actions was enough to SUPER INSPIRE me.

Afterwards, my mind was crazy with dreams and ideas. Because I am an extremely disciplined person—and was willing to do whatever it took to be successful and reach my goals—three years later, my husband was able to retire.

It all sounds easy, doesn't it? Remember I said that Diana Nyad accomplished her amazing swim only after four failed attempts? Before I was able to earn enough so that my husband could retire from construction, I had to reset my goal three times. But, like Diana Nyad, I was not about to give up. Even though I fell short of my goals several times, I never lost sight of them. I KNEW I had to achieve them.

While working for my company, another source of inspiration came my way. It was a book about habits of effective businesspeople written by bestselling author Stephen Covey. Here are the first two habits: Habit number one: be proactive in every aspect of your business. Habit number two: begin with the end in mind. I share these with you to inspire you! By the way, I recommend purchasing Mr. Covey's book *Seven Habits of Highly Effective People*, which is his worldwide bestseller, written for the general population.

Your Inspiration

Let's bring this chapter back to your life. It's time to seriously think about *what* inspires you and *who* inspires you. But where do you find the answers? For some people, they will come easily. Others may need some help.

What comes to mind when you think about something inspirational? Art? Scripture? A movie? A speech or a sermon? How about nature? I once visited the beautiful Niagara Falls with my daughter. I was absolutely in awe, as it was so breathtaking and inspiring. But the things that inspire aren't always "bigger than life." Even if the source is something as small as a mustard seed, when the wonder of it causes you to realize that life is bigger than who you are, it's inspiring.

Inspiration is something that you feel. It energizes you. It makes you feel proud. It drives you to accomplish goals. It lights a fire under you. It is something that causes you to reach for new levels you never thought you could attain.

One of the best ways to become inspired is to watch other people. When it comes to being inspired by people, there are examples all around. Think about those who sacrifice for the good of others; they are truly inspiring. They cause you to want to pattern your life after theirs. I'm inspired by Nelson Mandela, who spent 27 years in jail yet would not change his resolve to fight for equality and justice. I'm inspired by Gandhi; he achieved so much for the good of humanity without violence and bloodshed and without the use of an army or needed finances. I'm inspired by Christ, who actually loved us so much he gave his life. Such people inspire me to never give up. They inspire me to have the courage to face my battles and to stay strong in the midst of them.

When you see passion in other people, that's inspiring. How about the parents who leave their home country for another, so their children can have a better life than they did? Consider those who survived the Holocaust or escaped genocide or injustice in their own countries. These people have been through so much, yet many are alive to tell their stories. People from all walks of life who have survived natural disasters and national tragedies, and have overcome heartbreaking setbacks, inspire us to overcome our obstacles and to rise above our situations.

On a more personal level, I am inspired when I see my children and think about the legacy I want to leave. When I see my granddaughters, Kate, Esther and Hannah—I am blessed to have them carry on the legacy—they inspire me even more to accomplish everything I am supposed to do.

There is a reason we are here. Each one of us has a purpose in life that we are meant to fulfill. We need to live each and every day as if it were the last. And it is our responsibility to not just "go through the motions" but to inspire others through the legacy we leave behind.

Inspirational people show you that you don't necessarily need to "know someone" to accomplish your goals and dreams. With hard work, a little bit of luck, prayer, being in the right place at the right time, and taking every opportunity that comes your way, you can succeed in your chosen areas of life.

Diana Nyad certainly proved that. Her mantra was always "Find a way." To her words I would add, "Find a way to pursue your dreams."

You can also inspire yourself. Goal-setting is inspirational. Surpassing a previous level of success is inspirational. Achieving your desired level of monetary comfort for your family and/or yourself is inspirational.

Questions such as "What if?" and "Why?" can inspire you. Negative and critical comments from others can be inspirational. Have you ever had someone say, "You can't do that," and you replied, "Watch me"? Their words inspired you to do something you were not sure you could do.

Whether your source of inspiration is internal or external, it is really bigger than who you are. When you are inspired, you change. You grow. You become more than who or what you previously were.

I encourage you to take out a pad of paper, find a pen, and write down the names of everyone and everything that inspires you. Now take your list and put it somewhere you can read it every day, such as beside your bathroom mirror or on your refrigerator door. While you're at it, write your inspirations in your journal and record the reason(s) why this person or that thing is inspiring. Take the time to read your list at least a couple of times a week, and especially when you feel down. Your list will be a true pick- me-up and will be a source of inner strength. The more you read your inspirations, the more you will think, *Wow, I can gain strength from this/these.* Throughout your day, you will see the person or thing that inspires you in your mind's eye and think, *If he or she could do that, then I can accomplish my goals too.*

Whatever or whoever inspires you will help you live a fulfilling life on your own terms.

And living life to its fullest is the reason you are here. Diana Nyad is an Ambitious Woman.

You can be one too.

LIVE AN INSPIRED LIFE!

Chapter 2

Live an Encouraging Life

You CAN Make a Difference

Dr. Maya Angelou

When you think of the most encouraging person you know, who comes to mind? I have a couple. The first is an unknown housewife, and the second is a world- famous poet. Both of them are models of encouragement and sources of inspiration to me.

My mother was a stay-at-home mom, the unknown housewife. My father had a traditional job, working at a shoe factory. My father was a good father; unfortunately he was a victim of World War II. When he returned home from the battlefield, he had what was termed "shell shock." Today, we know this as Post Traumatic Stress Disorder [or possibly] manic depression, or bipolar disorder. When he was well and at home, he was the best and most loving father. But at least once every couple of years, he took a trip to the VA hospital and was gone for weeks and sometimes months. Thankfully, my wonderful and strong mother kept her family of four children together. Sometimes she went to work at the shoe factory because they were holding my dad's job. She was a constant source of encouragement to me. As of this writing, my 91-year-old mother is still a great encouragement to me.

The second woman who encourages me is Dr. Maya Angelou, poet, novelist, memoirist, novelist, educator, dramatist, producer, actress, historian, filmmaker. Now she was an Ambitious Woman! Despite being born into poverty and racial discrimination, despite being a single mother and high school dropout, and despite working as a cable car conductor and waitress, Dr. Angelou became one of the most renowned and influential voices of our time and was hailed as a global renaissance woman. She served on two presidential committees, was awarded the Presidential Medal of Arts in 2000 and the Lincoln Medal in 2008, and received three Grammy Awards. [2]

Sadly, this Renaissance woman passed away on May 28, 2014, but throughout her long life, she encouraged others, especially women of color, to become all that they could become. Her words and actions continue to stir our souls, energize our bodies, liberate our minds, and heal our hearts. She was an Ambitious Woman and her memory will continue to encourage entire generations to live life on their own terms and to overcome adversity in its many forms.

---

2 For more information on her life, visit http://mayaangelou.com/bio/

*****

My point in sharing these stories is that no matter what your family history might be, you can always look on the bright side of life. You just need someone to encourage you. That's what my mother did with all of her children. She kept the family together, even without my father present. She encouraged us that no matter what happened... we would make it.

That's what Dr. Maya Angelou did for countless thousands: encourage them to believe they could do it!

And it is what I hope I do with my life.

Encourage One Another

I love to encourage people. I've always encouraged others; it's a natural part of me. Because I believe being able to encourage others is a gift, I don't take credit for it; it is something that God has put inside of me. However, before I could be an encourager, I had to be encouraged myself ... and, as I said, it was my mother who was my first encourager.

Today, my greatest sources of encouragement are God, family, and friends.

The fact is, we all need encouraging. In order to know what that means, we need to have a clear understanding of the word "encourage." Webster's dictionary defines it this way: "to inspire with courage, spirit, or hope: hearten: to spur on: stimulate: to give help or patronage to: foster."

Let's get real here. It's very difficult to encourage yourself. I sometimes come across individuals who are down on themselves; they feel despondent and might even want to "throw in the towel." Now, it would be easy for me to say, "Hey, it's okay; tomorrow is a new day." But instead I've learned that to truly encourage people, it is best to listen first. Remind them that no matter what they are facing they can become better and stronger, if they choose to face their situations with a positive mindset.

I've learned that once you rise above your emotions, good things await you.

Sometimes encouragement has to be made with "tough love." You can say something like, "Hey, get over it!" to certain people, and they will receive your words because they know you love them. Or you can say, "You can do it, but it's your choice." That's a tough one because people don't want to hear that; they don't want to hear that they have to take responsibility. People would rather have you feel sorry for them, so be careful that you know the difference between encouraging and being an enabler.

To encourage one another goes hand-in-hand with inspiration and hope. In fact, ENCOURAGEMENT INSPIRES HOPE. Here is something to think about: At the heart of the word "encourage" is an encourager who cares. When you encourage friends, family members, or even strangers, you are showing them that you care about *who* they are and *what* they are going through. When we encourage others, we are making a personal connection; our hearts are reaching out to their hearts. In different forms and through various ways we are saying, "Come on, you can do it. And I'm here to cheer you on!"

For people with my personality—driven and perfectionistics—many times, it is easier to "go it alone." It is hard for us to admit we actually *need* someone else. Yet no matter what your personality, when you feel encouraged, your performance level rises; your resolve is strengthened; and, believe it or not, your overall health improves.

We often gain encouragement from others without knowing it. Like me, I'm sure you've had people say or do something for you, and you reply, "Thanks, I really needed that." Knowing someone is praying for you, receiving a card or email from a friend, even something as simple as a smile can greatly encourage us.

Encouragement is the reason we perform, sing, play an instrument, or do anything else in public. We are connecting with others in order to do our best, and we need the enthusiasm and the energy others bring into our lives. The applause we receive encourages us to do better. Whether at work, in a volunteer organization, in a church, or in business, if you want those who are under your guidance and care to succeed, you MUST encourage them as much as possible!

Encouraging other people tells them we are "in this" together. When we encourage others to achieve their goals, we give them courage and inspire them to "press on," even when the pressure is on.

An Encouraging Story

I read a lot, so I'm always looking for stories that I can share to help encourage others. I especially look for ones that make people think about themselves. Here's one from Jaise James's blog that makes a great point in a humorous way:

One day, not too long ago, the employees of a large company in Bangalore, India, returned from their lunch break and were greeted with a sign on the front door.

The sign read, "Yesterday, the person who has been hindering your growth in this company passed away. We invite you to join the funeral in the room that has been prepared in the gym."

At first everyone was sad to hear that one of their colleagues had died, but after a while they started getting curious about who this person might be. The excitement grew as the employees arrived at the gym to pay their last respects.

Everyone wondered, "Who is this person who was hindering my progress? Well, at least he's no longer here!"

One by one the employees got closer to the coffin and when they looked inside it, they suddenly became speechless. They stood over the coffin, shocked and in silence, as if someone had touched the deepest part of their soul.

There was a mirror inside the coffin: everyone who looked inside it could see himself. There was also a sign next to the mirror that said: "There is only one person who is capable to set limits to your growth: it is YOU."[3]

The point of the story is that YOU are the only person who can make the changes in your life that lead to happiness and success. The only way life changes is when *you* change. You are the one responsible for your life!

Reaching Out

Now I must admit, being an encourager is easy for people like me. For others it takes courage. You may be afraid of saying the wrong thing or even not know what to say. Sometimes words are not necessary. Just being there in someone's life can make a difference. How do you encourage someone?

Here are some things I've learned to do:

- Become aware of what encourages you, and do those same things for others.
- When you introduce someone, add a few words of praise for the person's abilities, accomplishments, how they've helped you, or about the nature of your relationship. It's encouraging to be praised in front of others.
- When someone is discouraged or hurting, offer specific, practical help. Say, "Would it help if I picked up your child from school?" or "I would like to bring by dinner tonight; is that okay?"

---

3 Excerpted from http://jaisejames.wordpress.com/2011/02/20/the-person-who-has-been-hindering-your-growth/

- Write someone a note, or text, send an email saying that you miss her/him, you just wanted to say hi, or something else that is encouraging.
- Celebrating is a great way to encourage others. Make celebration a regular part of your relationships. Celebrate the victories of others, large and small, with words, coffee together, a special meal, or a phone or text message.
- Be specific when you offer words of praise; it makes your encouragement more credible and concrete. "You did a great job at …" "I really appreciate that you …" "I was really impressed that you …"
- Realize the power of presence. Just being there for someone is encouraging! When you're with others, you're telling them they're important to you.
- If you're part of a larger group or community, your simple presence encourages others, even if you don't realize it.
- If someone you know is working long hours, or is a stay-at-home mom and overwhelmed with her life, send her flowers with an "I'm thinking of you" card.
- Write a letter or an email of encouragement to your boss or a co-worker.
- Tell the server he provided great service (if he really did).

- When you see people making positive changes in their lives, tell them. "You seem to have a really great attitude about ..." or "It may be that I'm just starting to take notice, but I see that you're ..." or "Do you think that you are becoming more ...?"
- Tell people how they've encouraged you!

Whom should you encourage? Everyone!

Encourage strangers. Tell them you love their dress, their jewelry. Say they have a great smile. It is so awesome to see strangers when you encourage or compliment them. I love it when strangers say something nice about my clothes, hair, or shoes. (It makes me want to go out and buy more shoes!) It just makes me feel good. So, go ahead and make someone's day! You have no ulterior motive, but your words will make them feel good and, in return, you will feel good.

I have a consultant in my business whose name is Visa. She will text me early in the morning several times a week and give me words of encouragement. She is always so positive with her life and her business, and that encourages me. Rarely have I seen her negative, even when things aren't going great. She is positive and has a stick-to-it attitude that I just love, and I am always encouraged by her! Perhaps being an encourager is what makes her so successful.

I have another friend, Leslie, who is a great encourager. She is always telling me to "go out" and do what she says I do best, "encourage and speak." She is one of my best cheerleaders and was a great source of encouragement when I started writing this book. She believed that I could do it before I believed I could.

Before we go to the next chapter, write down in your journal the names of the people you want to encourage, to remind you the next time you see them to go ahead and send a note and email, for no reason. You will see how much that encourages you.

Dr. Maya Angelou was an Ambitious Woman. You can be one too.

LIVE AN ENCOURAGING LIFE!

Chapter 3

Live an Action Life

Your Life Is Up to You

Mary C. Crowley

As well as shopping for shoes, I love to find things to make my home beautiful and personal. I have bought items from Home Interiors & Gifts for years, but I never gave much thought to the woman who founded the company. When I learned about her and her life, I knew she was the ideal example of an Ambitious Woman who TOOK ACTION and created the life of her dreams.

Mary C. Crowley was a single mom during the Depression.[4] She knew that if she and her children were to survive, she had to find a job. She did and, from her simple beginning, she honed business skills that helped her found a multimillion-dollar business created to help women decorate beautiful homes at a reasonable price. Her company, Home Interiors & Gifts, provided career opportunities for

4 Read more about her life at: www.historyswomen.com/1stWomen/Mary-Crowley.html

women to enhance their lives through decorating the homes and lives of others. Her home accessory line was one of the largest sellers of home decorative accessories in the United States.

Mary Crowley was an Ambitious Woman! She fought two bouts with cancer but continued on. In 1977, she was one of twenty business leaders invited to a conference with President Carter. She was the first woman to serve on the board of directors of the Billy Graham Evangelistic Association. She received two honorary doctorate degrees before her death in 1986. Incidentally, she is the grandmother of Joey Carter, and the mother of Don Carter (yes, *the* Carters of the Dallas Mavericks); it was her actions that helped create a basketball legacy. She definitely took action in her life.

*****

How do you "take action"? How much action do you need to take? What are the best actions to take to achieve your desired results? In short, what does living an "action-based life" mean to you as an Ambitious Woman?

It Starts with You

As someone who takes ACTION, I know where I am going and what I want to do, but sometimes I get stuck in the "How am I going to do this?" phase. When I contemplate this question, I realize everything begins with the choices I'm making at that particular moment. And a lot of those choices involve *inaction*!

I might be waiting on someone else to take the initiative. It's possible that I want to blame someone or something else for my inactivity. I might be waiting for that "perfect" way to do something, even though I know that the "perfect way" will only come about if I start doing what I need to do.

The first step in taking charge is to realize that everything begins with you: You must take responsibility. This does not mean yelling, "Get out of my way; I'll get it done!" Instead, taking responsibility means you are willing to be responsible for the final outcome. While others may come alongside you to help, you are willing to be responsible for them, sharing ideas, teaching them, and learning from them. In business, there is an acronym that successful people learn early on. TEAM: Together, Each Achieves More. So go ahead and take the responsibility that you need to. By taking charge, you, and everyone around you, will benefit.

How I Took Charge

When my husband, Frank, and I lived in San Diego, we owned a contracting company for over 15 years and, sometime into it, I started a business that marketed baby products. It started when I found the perfect bib for my third son, Peter, at a craft fair. I loved it. However, I couldn't find it in any store when I wanted another one. So I decided to design, sew, package, and sell my own "Bib Over Bib" through my own company. (This was before buying on the Internet was even thought of!) It took off and soon I was marketing other baby products as well. "Charming Baby Products" were all invented by real moms and dads from real needs they found while raising babies!

It was a great time. Our ceramic tile company was one of the top five largest in San Diego, and my baby business was booming—until the recession of the 90s hit. We had thought that we were going to be successful forever and never run out of money. But then construction stopped, and the upscale baby business went to the wayside as well.

This period of time was the most humbling experience I have ever gone through. I thought, *Wow, from the top of my game to bottom of the barrel.* I questioned God daily. *Why is he letting this happen? We've been faithful; we've tithed and given faithfully.*

During those difficult years in San Diego, I could have easily given up and allowed depression to take over my life. But I didn't. I believe everything happens for a reason. Life has a way of turning out, if you allow it. I took charge in every area I could. I had four little kids, and I needed to be responsible for them. I had other people depending on me, and I needed to take action. That meant getting other jobs just to pay the bills and put food on the table. I had to do whatever it took to survive. I even remember selling solar pools, commission only, my first attempt at sales, after being an owner with over 100 employees and living the good life. Now, I was out there all alone, trying to sell something I didn't know anything about. It was very humbling, to say the least.

But, by staying strong and taking action, we were soon given the opportunity to move to Texas and start over.

Take Action and Take Charge

To me, taking action and taking charge is a mindset, but they may mean different things to different people. So I'd like to share with you some of the things I think this means.

Taking charge means taking responsibility, even when a situation is not your fault. It is easy to play the "blame game." Yes, people need to be held accountable for their actions, but blaming others and circumstances have no part in that. Finding fault is all about looking backwards, while taking responsibility and saying, "What can we do to fix this?" is looking forward. When we focus on responsibility, we can create an atmosphere of peace.

It wasn't my family's fault the recession happened. We didn't cause it, but we were part of it, and so we could either be buried in it or take action and do whatever we had to do to keep going. Did changes happen overnight? No, it was many years later that we finally recovered, but we learned many things through those trying times and are better people because of what we went through. Sometimes taking action starts with something concrete, like writing down goals, ideas, directions, or plans. Writing these things out helps us to envision how to take action—the best course of action.

Taking charge means that we must "stay in the present." It is easy to daydream, to let our minds wander, to doodle away on a notepad. But when we force ourselves to do the task at hand, it helps us to not "over-think" and just do what needs to be done.

Now here's a question that can make a big difference in wanting to take action and in actually taking action: Are you really doing what you need to do right now, at this moment, in this situation?

Taking the action you need to do right now involves being accountable to others. When we tell others what we are going to do, it is hard not to follow through because others are depending on us to keep our word. Accountability helps us develop consistency and good habits. Sometimes we don't want to share our goals and plans, because if we do and then don't follow through or we fail, no one will know. It makes things that much easier.

Or does it?

Even if no one else knows, you will always know what you didn't do. And you will know you are not growing as an Ambitious Woman. At the end of your life, the most important person will know that you didn't do what you could have done ... YOU are that person.

For some people, the very thought of taking charge can feel overwhelming. That's where writing a SHORT to- do list comes in handy. A short list allows you to check things off; and a fully checked-off list will do wonders for your mental health.

Think about the two or three most important things you want to accomplish—not the big-picture things, but the smaller things you know you can finish—and focus on these. The list will seem less overwhelming, and I have found that it makes it much easier to take action.

While we are at it, take out your journal, and begin your SHORT list. What are the two or three things you need to do now? Write them down. Take action to get them done. Then make another short list. You'll soon find that you will be able to make a longer list and tackle it without stress.

The Flip Side

Are you someone who takes life "too seriously"? There are times when you simply need to take a break or lighten up. For my fellow goal-oriented sisters who are reading this book, this is a big one. Taking a break can actually do us a lot of good. When we come back to the task at hand, we see things in a different light, which can make taking charge a little easier.

Here's an example of what I'm talking about from my life.

My favorite getaway is the beach. But I am considered by many, including my own family, to be a bit of a workaholic (okay, a lot of a workaholic!). I do love to work; it's my passion. However, when I need to take a break, or to take some time to lighten up, I head for the beach … there's something about the water that just relaxes me without even trying. I was used to being at the beach within twenty minutes when we lived in San Diego, but when we moved to Texas, the nearest beach was seven hours away! I don't think I saw the beach for the first five years we lived here. But one day, after I had been working at my new business, I decided to head to the beach and expand my business there! I bought a condo in Corpus Christi, two blocks from the beach, and every time I go over the bridge onto the island I am a different person! (Not to mention Leslie lives there!)

It's Up to You

I want to tell you upfront: You CAN do it! Whatever you have planned, from daily household duties to big-picture ideas, if you want to live a life of purpose and have fulfillment, it's up to you to make it happen.

Is it going to be easy? No, but it's going to be worth it. And it will help you live an exponentially more interesting and fulfilling life. Remember, no more excuses; no more whining; no more looking at what hinders you and allowing it to stop you in your tracks. Don't give up, but reclaim what is rightfully yours to do. Tell yourself, "I'm going to take back what is rightfully mine." Remember, everyone has fears, everyone has failed, and everyone is a procrastinator at some point. But these don't have to hold you back. Take charge of your life and live to the fullest each and every day!

So, TAKE ACTION! In fact, TAKE MASSIVE ACTION!

Mary Crowley was an Ambitious Woman. You can be one too.

LIVE AN ACTION LIFE!

Chapter 4

Live Your Dream Life

If You Can Dream It, You Can Live It

Susan Boyle

The judges on *Britain's Got Talent* could barely keep from rolling their eyes when the contestant stepped on the stage. Simon Cowell used his most patronizing tone of voice when he asked the dowdy brunette what her goal was. His smirk turned to shock, and then stunned admiration, when she began to sing "I Dreamed a Dream" from *Les Miz*. In that moment 48-year-old Susan Boyle's dream of being a famous singer came true. In fact, her debut album was the most pre-ordered album worldwide of all time at Amazon before its global release.[5]

I remember the first time I watched Susan Boyle sing. I was speechless. In fact, I actually fought back tears. Such a pure voice. Such an unassuming woman. Such humility. Yet I also saw something else in her: she was an Ambitious Woman. She was ambitious enough to put aside all of her fears

5 For more information, see http://www.susanboylemusic.com/us/story/

and insecurities to live out her dream. To this day, all I can say is "Wow!" whenever I hear her songs. If you want to find encouragement to live out your dreams, go to YouTube and listen to her audition night. I guarantee that you will be fighting back tears too!

*****

Apple founder Steve Jobs said in a 2005 commencement address at Stanford University, "Your time is limited, so don't waste it living someone else's life. Don't be trapped by dogma—which is living with the results of other people's thinking. Don't let the noise of others' opinions drown out your own inner voice. And most important, have the courage to follow your heart and intuition. They somehow already know what you truly want to become. Everything else is secondary."[6] I often think about this quote during my week; it helps me to create my own vision, knowing that I have to forge my own path in life.

Most all of us have dreams, ambitions, goals or aspirations ... at least of some kind. Things we want to do or become. But sometimes life can get in the way, can't it? We may have great intentions but the drudgery of the day- to-day, the responsibilities and the busyness, can leave us merely trying to survive ... much less give us any margin to thrive. Days turn into weeks and weeks turn into years, and if we aren't careful we can find ourselves living but not being truly alive.

---

6 http://www.huffingtonpost.com/2011/10/05/steve-jobs-stanford- commencement-address_n_997301.html

Brian McClure, a network marketing guru, and one of the top earners in the world, calls this "someday thinking." He found himself for years telling his young son, "Someday I'm going to take you fishing." "Someday we're going to do this or that." It was always "someday." But someday never happened until he finally decided the "someday" needed to be NOW.

Do you have any "someday" dreams? I think most of us—maybe all of us—do. The good news though is that someday dreams can become TODAY'S REALITY. As an Ambitious Woman, you CAN DO ANYTHING … anything you choose to do. We have a mantra in our business that I have had from the beginning: "Some people dream, some make dreams happen." The great thing is, we all get to choose which person we want to be!

I've known women from all walks of life including highly successful leaders, entrepreneurs, business women, and everyday moms. They are all successful because they LIVE THEIR LIVES ON PURPOSE and according to the dreams they have for their lives. These people are not necessarily smarter, better looking, or more privileged than the rest of us. Instead, they see the world and their lives through their own eyes. They have a unique perspective on life, and they are not deterred by others trying to get them to see a different way of life.

A Personal Challenge

I think we all have a secret dream. But that dream seems

so far away that we can't imagine how it could ever happen. And we fear that if we talk about the dream, we will be ridiculed and someone will rip our precious dream apart. Because of this fear, we never even think about turning the dream into a reality. Fear tells us that it must always stay a dream; we must not even think about the possibilities.

So, I'm going to challenge you to do what seems so scary.

Take a few minutes and think about these questions:

- What is your wildest dream?
- What do you really want to do?
- Who do you really want to be?

Let your imagination flow. Be creative. Let yourself dream.

If you are like most people, you really haven't considered this question before. Most people are stuck in the status quo. They are living life, but not to its fullest. Why? Because our wildest dreams are scary; they seem too big to accomplish. So put aside your fears, and let me ask you again, "What is your wildest dream? The one that seems too big; the one that you don't even confide to your best friend."

People tend not to share their dreams and aspirations. That's because if they do share, and they don't achieve their dream or goal, no one will know. It is much easier to not tell anyone rather than look like a failure, but that is not the way to live.

I know; I used to be that way.

It started when I was in the seventh grade, and I had a dream to be a cheerleader at school. I wanted to be popular, and I thought that would be a good way. But I was afraid of not making it, of failing. So I didn't tell my parents, who could have encouraged me. That way if I didn't make the squad, they wouldn't know. I applied on my own, I practiced on my own, and I went to the tryout on my own. It was all secret. Well, I made the first cut with the judges. But then came the voting, and the students would decide the cheerleaders by popular vote. Guess what? I didn't make it. Whew! I was relieved I hadn't told my parents. Now they never had to know about my secret dream. I did that a lot growing up and in my early adult life. With that type of thinking, all I had was dreams; I never saw anything become reality.

Once I started to read books and learn about personal development, my thinking changed and I saw what I was doing—I was not living my dreams. I was sabotaging them from the beginning.

What Hinders Your Dreams?

You might have read books about "pursuing your dreams." One of my personal favorite books is *Dream to Destiny* by my pastor, Robert Morris. He talks about the ten tests that we must go through to fulfill God's purpose for our lives, using the story of Joseph in the Bible. Even though I learned to pursue my dreams, it was life changing to understand that each of us actually has a destiny. The problem is that most of us do not do what the books say to do. If we did, we would be out there, bringing reality to our dreams and visions. I think we all know what to do; we just need to DO IT. But what about the things that do not allow you to pursue your dream? What about the things that really do hinder you? As I thought about these questions, I realized that most people *want* to accomplish their dreams, but they don't know what to do about the things that hinder them. So I would like to share the top three things that I have learned to overcome—what I call "The 3 Don'ts."

1. **Don't Listen to Dream Stealers.** No matter who they are or how close they are to you, don't let others steal your dreams. Whatever your dream is, it's important to be careful with whom you share it. Confide only in people who will support you unconditionally. Whether they truly believe in your dream is not as important as the fact that they BELIEVE IN YOU! Those who tell you, "That will never work," are afraid to follow their own dreams. They just don't have the wherewithal that you do. It takes courage and focus to follow your dreams to reality.

   One of the great lessons from the Bible illustrates this point. There is a story about a woman who had a bleeding disorder for twelve years. She had suffered under many doctors and spent her life savings. Yet when she heard about Jesus, she was determined to get close to him. Even if she could touch only the hem of his robe, she believed that would be enough to be healed. She didn't let her "past" stop her; she didn't let "lack" stop her; and she didn't let the crowds stop her. She had a mindset to get what she needed. She fought through the crowds and she was healed. Now that is an Ambitious Woman!

When my son David was in college, he was constantly pursuing his dreams. One day, he sent me a quote that he made up: "I Fail to Let Myself Fail." Wow, that's pretty profound, even for a college student. Even today he "fails to let himself fail." He is an amazing entrepreneur and dream chaser; he doesn't let ANYONE steal his dreams.

2. **Don't Worry About Failing.** Now, this doesn't contradict what David said. The point here is that most people are so caught up trying *not* to fail that they paralyze themselves with fear. This is something David simply does not do. If something doesn't work out, he finds a different way of doing it. That's not failure. The only real failure is to stop trying.

   Fear of failure is the ultimate dream stealer. Here are some truths:

   - If you don't fail, you won't learn.
   - Failure is the road to success.
   - Failing keeps you moving forward on the right path towards success.
   - Here's a great quote from Thomas Edison: "I have not failed. I've just found 10,000 ways that won't work." What a great attitude is that!

In my line of business, we have a saying: "Race to 100 No's." You have to have a certain amount of No's to get a Yes. So instead of being upset or discouraged when you get a no, celebrate it! You are that much closer to a YES!

If you have enough failures, you are bound to be that much closer to a success! I have had more failures than successes in my life. Some people don't know that. They look at me and think I have *always* been successful. No way! I have started, tried, and pursued dozens of endeavors: Some produced limited success, and some just right out failed. When my husband and I finally had a successful tile business, I thought we had made it, only to have it fail later on. But we kept pursuing our dream of financial freedom.

Finally, after years of trial and error, I achieved the kind of success in business I had dreamed about. All those failures prepared me to be successful. I can honestly say those are truthful words. I didn't believe it when I read it years ago, or when people told me how your failures will help you, but now I know they do! However, I believe I have yet to achieve my greatest success. I am just getting started!

3. **Don't Give Up.** Please hear my words; bind them to your mind: *Don't give up until your dreams come true!* If you give up, who else will accomplish what you had in mind to do? YOU are the only one who can do that.

When you are tempted to give up, go back to the reason

why you started down the path you are on in the first place.

Here's a great real life example. Adam and Michelle are a sweet young couple that pursued their dreams and didn't give up. They started their business in California, but they knew if they were going to be successful, they would have to move to Texas, where most of the business was at the time. So they packed up their pick-up truck with all their belongings and moved. Once in Texas, they found part time jobs to supplement their income while they built their business. Michelle was a waitress and Adam a CEO (Car Expert Organizer) … in other words, he parked cars. They did it because they knew about "delayed gratification." They were willing to sacrifice in the beginning so that later they could accomplish their dream of financial freedom and being stay-at-home parents. Well six years later, they had established a successful business, and they were able to move back to their home and families in California. After pursuing their dreams, Hannah Grace was born on April 15, 2014, and they are stay-at-home parents with her. (Not to mention Michelle was able to pay off all of her seven credit cards.) But that happened because they never gave up! Was it always easy? Of course not. But if they would have given up, they would have given up on their dream!

When I first started with my business in Texas, one of my goals was to retire my husband after working all those years in the construction industry. But I also wanted to have my OWN retirement money as well. That's why I got up every day and did not give up until my dreams became a reality. Three-and-a-half years later, my husband laid his last ceramic tile. And I still don't give up because I want to be able to buy all the shoes I want!

Follow Your Dreams

Some dreams are big, others are small. But no matter the size of your dream, here are three things to always keep in mind:

Believe. Whatever you dream, whatever your idea, it comes from your core being and it is part of what you are supposed to accomplish in life. So believe in it. Believe that you are MORE than capable of achieving it (no matter what anyone else tells you). It is part of the unique calling that God has placed on your life. If you don't go after it, then you're not living the life that you were intended to live and you will feel out of balance, as if something is missing. Whatever you are dreaming about, when you begin to bring it into reality, you will be amazed at the resources and the people who will materialize to help you. That doesn't mean your path to success will be easy; after all no dream worth living was ever accomplished without hard work, persistence, and determination. If you haven't read the book *Break Out* by Joel Osteen, now would be a good time to read it. Believe that you are ready to break out! And it will happen!

Stop Waiting for Perfection. Perfection is a myth, and you will never achieve it. You're kidding yourself if you are waiting for the perfect time, the perfect place, or the perfect sign. If we all waited for the perfect time, none of us would have children and the world would never be populated. Waiting on perfection is just an excuse to procrastinate and give in to the fear that tries to limit you. Success requires doing. It's great to think and plan, ponder, and perfect. But if you overthink, you can easily reach the point of inaction. If you don't "do" you'll end up wishing you did.

Start Today with Tomorrow in Mind. Whatever you want to achieve, remember that you cannot "sprint" there; more than likely you'll feel like you are in a marathon. I once heard a businessman say, "It's taken me ten years to achieve overnight success." That's true for most of us. All great sculptors, all great artists, and all great architects envision exactly what they want to see before they ever start. When my husband, Frank, was a tile contractor, one thing he enjoyed about that business was the end result. He could look at a shabby floor, bathtub, kitchen counter, or fireplace and envision how beautiful it would look when he was done.

I have a big sign in my outdoor bathroom by the pool. (Don't ask me why I put it in the bathroom. I guess I just want people to be inspired when they are in there!) It reads: "DREAM (noun): a longing or aspiration created by the heart, meant to be pursued!" That is so true!

Incidentally, when you dream, always dream about the end result. A few years ago, a friend and I were sunning on the beach. I glanced over at her, and she was reading a book. When I noticed the name of the book she was reading I asked, "Hey, why aren't you sharing this with me?" Instead of a book being about how to look young— which is unrealistic by the way—this one was about how NOT to look old! What a great concept. Instead of learning what to do, how about learning what NOT to do? By the way, if you want to pick up the book, it is called *How Not to Look Old: Fast and Effortless Ways to Look 10 Years Younger, 10 Pounds Lighter, 10 Times Better* by Charla Krupp. Now that's ambitious!

Now what is your dream? What vision do you have? Take out your journal and write out your "someday" dreams. Remember, only you can accomplish what is in your heart. There is no one else who can do what you do. So go out and do it! LIVE YOUR DREAM and you'll fulfill your destiny!

Susan Boyle is an Ambitious Woman. You can be one too.

LIVE YOUR DREAMS!

Chapter 5

Live a Determined Life

You Can Make A Difference

Manal Elzeen

Manal Elzeen and her family left Sudan to seek asylum in the United States, resettling in Fort Wayne, Indiana. Before leaving her country, Manal taught high school economics and accounting. Now she uses her financial background and expertise to operate her own family childcare business. Despite the difficulties involved with coming to a new country and starting over, Manal says, "If you want to get anywhere in this life you need to work hard and learn more. This is an opportunity to receive the support needed to be successful. I want to make my business great!"[7]

You don't have to be born in a first world country to be an Ambitious Woman. Women such as Manal Elzeen show that determination is a mindset, a heart condition: one that we can choose for ourselves, no matter where we live. Manal

7 Manal Elzeen and daughter, and picture found at and excerpted from http://www.acf.hhs.gov/programs/orr/success-story/determination-and-hard-work-pays-off

Elzeen is an Ambitious Woman!

*****

Determine to Be Determined

Determination means to be intent on achieving a goal. We all face obstacles, roadblocks, trials, and tribulations in life. But the question is: What are we going to do about them? We must "determine to be determined." This simple decision will give us the energy, the focus, and the drive to accomplish our goals.

For as long as I can remember, I've been a determined person. For instance, I always wanted to be the teacher when I played school with my two sisters and the other neighborhood kids. I made the rules, and I was determined to teach the class.

Determination has different meanings for different people. For some, it means to have a strong intention or a fixed intention. For others, it means they have strong willpower. Still others see determination as a strong sense of self-devotion and self-commitment. For my then two-year-old grandson, Owen, determination is staying tough enough to defend himself from his older siblings and cousins bugging him. All of these people and little "Owie" have one thing in common: They have decided to achieve their objectives, no matter what their personal histories tells them, no matter what those who are currently in their lives tell them, and no matter how bleak the future might look.

They are determined to succeed.

My System to Stay Determined

Being in business for yourself is not an easy path to take. And I'm sure the path you have chosen is not easy either. So I'd like to share with you three things that will help you to stay determined.

Make a Decision ONE Time. Decide the path you are going to take, and don't waver. There is no turning back. While your life might not change in the next 30, 60, or 100 days, or even within the next year, nevertheless, stick with your decision. I tell people who are starting a new business or new endeavor that they should make a two-year commitment, or at least persevere until the desired goal has been reached, before ever thinking of going in another direction. Don't give up midway if you determined a time frame.

When I first started my business, I decided that if I was going to be successful in it, I was going to have to embrace my new career. So I put my heels on, dressed up, put signs on my car (which previously I only thought nerds did), and started attending chamber and networking groups so that I could meet other business people. I knew what I had to do if I wanted to be successful, so I did it.

Decide EXACTLY What You Want to Accomplish. In my case, this was an easy decision but one that was very hard to do. I wanted to make enough money to retire my husband and have enough money to pay all the bills … and, of course, buy shoes. I did that and more. Now,

I don't recommend that everyone aim to make millions (unless that's truly your goal), but knowing exactly what you want will keep you on the "straight and narrow" when tangents come your way. You have to decide exactly what you want and then do it! Something happens when you just do what you're supposed to do; you are able to do the impossible. I decided early on, if I was going to accomplish my goals, then I would have to share my business with as many people as I could. Now this may not apply to what you are going to do, but when you figure out what you want to accomplish, it is much easier to find out how you will go about fulfilling your goals.

NEVER GIVE UP. There it is again. The "never give up" statement! But it is so true. The underlying mindset of every characteristic of the Ambitious Woman is "Never give up!" Bottom line, NEVER, EVER, EVER GIVE UP! Don't give up on your dreams … determination will help you achieve them!

Lessons Learned

My first introduction to being an entrepreneur was in the late 70s. Frank and I saw an ad in the paper about making extra money, and we decided to attend the seminar. Well, it was about raising worms and selling them. Believe it or not, we thought this was a great idea. We bought two beds of worms for $750.00 each and the food to feed them. (Even now that is a lot of money!) At home, we constructed a 6-foot x 8-foot wood bed full of dirt and mulch for the worms. The idea was that in 60 days they would multiply, giving us four beds. They in turn would multiply into eight, then sixteen, then thirty-two beds … you get the picture. Well, we got up to sixteen beds and were spending hundreds of dollars keeping these worms fed. The idea was to sell them to a company that used them to eat garbage. We finally got our friends to buy two beds and we made money on that, but NOT the worms! The company we were working with went out of business. So Frank and I got rid of our beds of worms and that was that. However, I found something I loved doing: being an entrepreneur. And I was determined to find a business I could succeed at.

*****

Manal Elzeen is a determined and Ambitious Woman, but one of the most determined people I know is my very own niece, Janelle Cline. Janelle has built a huge business from the North Pole, Alaska. Yes, that's right, the North Pole, as in Santa Claus lives there. She was determined from the beginning to make her business work. She made a decision, she decided exactly what she wanted to accomplish, and … she never gave up! Janelle was a highly successful civil engineer for ten years, but then wanted to be a stay-at-home mom with her two girls. After four years persevering to build her network in creative ways, she has now retired from her civil engineering job. She was an entrepreneur by heart—I always told her, "You were never really an engineer, but an entrepreneur just trying to get out."

In her own words …

"Success is not an accident. Those who accomplish great things in life have what I call a 'can-do' attitude—they are determined to can-do whatever is needed to accomplish their goals. They are optimistic, have a sense of purpose, are passionate about what they do, are persistent and determined, and believe in themselves. All of these qualities allow them to persevere in the face of all setbacks and overcome obstacles. The key to determination comes from being committed to your goal, connecting with your purpose, and visualizing your goal's possibility. Determination builds strength through persistence and often hinges on your ability to be consistent with your efforts by refocusing on your goal again and again, day in and day out. You have to be willing to pay the price, for as long as it takes, until you achieve the results you desire. If you are determined, you will succeed."

Now, take out your journal and just write down ONE thing that you determine to pursue and stay with it until you succeed. If you are DETERMINED, you can do it!

Manal Elzeen and Janelle Cline are Ambitious Women.

You can be one too.

LIVE A DETERMINED LIFE!

Chapter 6

Live an Empowered Life

What You Do Makes a Difference

Empowered women aren't always the most famous or the most visible. But they are the Ambitious Women who make a difference in the world. That's because empowered women act on their own initiative and do what has to be done, without waiting for someone to come along and tell them what to do.

My sister, Betsy, who wrote the foreword for this book, is an empowered woman. Her husband of 35 years, Lee, was a master craftsman, and she worked in the criminal justice department in Palmer, Alaska. They had just built their retirement home and life was good. Then the unexpected happened: Lee was diagnosed with a terminal illness and given six months to live. She had thought about working with me after Lee passed away; she had to find a way to support herself, as she had lost all of Lee's income. After joining my company, she eventually was able to sell her home in Alaska and move to Texas. What a great feeling for me that I was able to empower her with the belief that she could take care of herself and live the life she wanted ... IF she believed she could. She was empowered!

Remember Adam and Michelle, the young couple who left their roots in California to pursue their dream in Texas … and succeeded? That was empowerment!

I think of my friends and business owners, Terry and Melanie, who because of this last recession in California lost their home, business, finances, even their ability to earn income. What would you do if you were in your 60s and had to start over? Terry and Melanie figured out a way to do just that and now have new hope and residual income for themselves, their children, and their grandchildren. They are empowered!

I am grateful to have played a part in empowering these people and so many more to go for the life they've always wanted to live!

A Better Life

One issue that often gets in the way of creating our "best life" is that we don't know what we don't know. However, when someone empowers us— through knowledge, understanding, wisdom, permission, and more—we can learn the difference between "coping" or "managing" life and "creating" and "living" the life we want for ourselves; the life each of us deserves.

When we empower people through our words, actions, or attitudes, we give them the ability to direct and control their own lives. Now that might seem strange, but I often come across people who feel lost, hopeless, and ready to give up. But who we are, what we say, and what we do can give others hope to live and to move on with their lives. Empowering others allows them to begin to recognize they have choices in life. It moves them from talking about what they can only *wish* for to concrete actions. In return, you become an empowered woman and will become an even more Ambitious Woman.

Some people have lived lifetimes of bondage. Whether to their own mindsets, habits, and actions, or in true physical bondage, these people simply drift through life, not knowing there really is something "better out there." Or if they do know this, they feel it is so far beyond their reach, it might as well be a dream that never comes true. However, when we help empower these people, we move them from feeling powerless through that to feeling empowered. We can help them begin to understand that they can create the life they want, no matter what others have told them.

Empowering Mindsets

It is easy to feel empowered when your life is headed in the right direction, and when you are accomplishing your goals and dreams. But we all come to points in our lives when we are falling short, when we don't feel we can move forward. Worse, sometimes we don't have anyone around us to encourage us and to reignite the power within us. If you find yourself in that position—currently or in the future—I would like to be the one who empowers you once again.

In 1994, when my family and I lost everything, then moved to Texas, I felt like a complete failure. Over ten years of hard work in California had just gone down the drain. What would I do? How could I start over?

Throughout my life, the Bible has been the single greatest source of my empowerment. It offers so much fundamentally sound advice. My favorite book is the Book of Proverbs. If you have never read the Bible, I encourage you to read a chapter of Proverbs a day for 30 days, and you will find so much business, family, and spiritual truth imparted to you. I try to do this at least once a year.

As I mentioned before, I love to read. I always have from the moment I could read in the first grade. I think that reading is one of my biggest sources of empowerment. When I read books by John Maxwell, the great leadership guru, I am empowered. One of his books is titled, *Sometimes You Win, Sometimes You Learn.* I encourage you to get the book! But even if you only make the book title a part of your mindset, it will no doubt empower you when you face times of doubt.

When we face times of delays, when we face trials and tribulations, these often serve to "sap our power." But if we look at these times with the right perspective, they can actually empower us. For example, we learn to be more patient, we learn that we really aren't in control, we learn to be faithful, to be humble, and to be compassionate; these are life-changing, and they can empower us to keep moving on in the face of difficult situations.

These are just a few of the lessons I've learned through my hard times.

Here is another empowering statement that I learned from one of my mentors, and now a family friend, Bill Clarke: "Successful people do what unsuccessful people do not." I believe that is the ONE difference between successful people and unsuccessful people, bottom line. Bill was my manager and he taught me everything I know today about sales, which became my foundation to the success in my own business. He empowered me daily by telling me I COULD do it, even when I didn't think I could keep going

… even through all the disappointments, all the no's.

I also did things to empower myself. When I first started the job, we had just moved to Texas and the only vehicle I had was the 1970 Dodge van that my family had driven across the country; it looked like a hippie van. We had traded it for eight acres of land in San Diego, just to have transportation. That is how bad life was. When we finally settled down in Texas, I knew that if I was going to be successful, I wouldn't be able to drive to clients in that 1970 Dodge van, WITHOUT air conditioning no less. I remember Bill telling me later on that on my first day of work, he looked out of his fourth floor window and watched me get into that van. He thought to himself, "She's not going to make it." But you know what? I found a way to make it! Just like Diana Nyad's mantra "Find a Way" I found a used Cadillac and got the owner to take payments. Even though I was broke as anything, I felt empowered when I drove that Caddy! It gave me the empowerment to be SUCCESSFUL! But, there was a lot of work I still had had to do.

At the time I was doing this commission-only sales job, and I had a quota to reach if I wanted to keep my job. It was tough. Fifty phone calls daily, 20 cold calls daily, and 250 drop off stuffers weekly! I was told these were the things I would have to do in order to be successful. This is what I needed to do EVERY DAY if I wanted to be successful, so I did it. Guess what? Most of the other people that were hired at the same time or came after me must not have wanted to be successful because they never met their quota, and they quit.

Remember this: Successful people do what unsuccessful people will NOT do. Think about this mindset. Everyone wants to be successful, but not everyone is willing to do what it takes. Unless you are fortunate enough to have a successful business or other endeavor handed to you, you are starting with your dreams and visions. You then have to have the attitude of "Whatever it takes."

You might want to have a successful speaking career or start a ministry or other non-profit. You may want to start a family and raise your kids according to your faith and beliefs. If you know you are good at something, keep in mind the world doesn't know that. So you have to prove yourself. I always keep in mind that it is God who promotes me, in his timing and according to his will for my life. But I still have to do my part.

Words to Live By

Throughout my life, I've learned some great self- empowering and others-empowering lessons. Some have come naturally to me, others I have learned the hard way. I pass these along to you, trusting that they will empower you too.

- Empowering others means I don't criticize. That doesn't mean I don't address things I feel needed to be addressed, but I try to do so in a non-condemning way.
- Empowering others means I don't judge. It is so easy to judge the motives of others, but we don't live their lives.
- Empowering others means I am not cynical. For people like me who are perfectionists, it is easy to develop a cynical attitude. But we must resist!
- Resist others means praising. No matter if it is a kind word, a smile, or any other form of praise, when we praise others we truly do "light up their worlds."
- Empowering others means curbing my ego. Wow, now that's a big one for all of us!
- Empowering others means being your best. When others see me at my best, they feel they can do their best as well.
- **Empowering others means others feel they are loved.** I bolded this one because it is THE most important thing you can do for others—and yourself.

Now, think about the people in your life closest to you.

Think of how you might be able to empower their lives. Write their names down in your journal. If you help enough people get what they want, you will get what you want.

*****

Recently, I heard a man once say, "Men have strength, but women have power!"

I believe we all have special characteristics in us that we haven't unleashed yet. Maybe because we just haven't had the right opportunity to. When you want something so bad is when you will have the power to take control. When you are so passionate about something that it keeps you awake at night, that's when your special qualities will surface. These qualities will empower you to strive to be better, empower you to do more than you ever thought was possible, and empower you to believe in yourself when no one else does.

Empowerment is an action word and to me empowerment means taking control. I didn't realize I was being empowered and taking control because I was so focused on the task at hand. But looking back now, that's exactly what was happening. To put it simply, to be empowered is to stay focused on what you want out of life and believe that you deserve it and can achieve it because you will never stop working towards it. Whatever you desire, it is yours! Go for it, you can do it!"

*****

When we feel empowered we can change our worlds. When others feel empowered, they can change their worlds. And change always makes the world a better place to live!

Betsy is an Ambitious Woman

You can be one too.

LIVE AN EMPOWERED LIFE!

Chapter 7

Live a Motivated Life

Understand What Drives You To Succeed

Nancy Brinker

What would you do if your sister died from breast cancer at age 36? Nancy G. Brinker founded Susan G. Komen for the Cure® to honor her sister. The organization is now at the vanguard of breast cancer cure and research. When she began her journey, people didn't even like to say the words "breast cancer" out loud. Today, Susan G. Komen is the world's largest grassroots network of breast cancer survivors and activists fighting to save lives, empower people, ensure quality care for all, and energize science to find the cures. In 2009, President Barack Obama honored her with the Presidential Medal of Freedom, the nation's highest civilian honor, for her work and she was named one of TIME magazine's "100 Most Influential People."

You cannot help but admire Nancy Brinker. Almost every woman in our country has been affected by breast cancer, either through their own battles, or by supporting loved ones, friends, and co-workers who have faced this hideous disease. But with people like Nancy championing the cause, the cure for breast cancer cannot be far away. Nancy Brinker is not only motivated; she is an Ambitious Woman!

*****

You have to be a motivated woman if you are going to be an Ambitious Woman. Most women are already motivated, especially when it comes to their families.

We wear our Superwoman cape and proclaim we can do all the necessary jobs at work and home—and more—all at once? Someone sent me a cartoon picture one time, and they said it reminded them of me. A woman was eating an apple, putting on makeup, talking on the cell, listening to the radio, all while driving the car. Now while that might be a slight exaggeration, and certainly not safe, that could be a picture of many of us.

Sources of Motivation

What, exactly, are you motivated to do? I want to really dig into this topic. It is so key to everything we do. One way to truly figure this out is to understand that "motivation" should be based on what we are enthused about. Enthusiasm *should* drive the choices we make. Of course, we are motivated by obligation, responsibility, even avoidance of emotional or physical pain (except when we go to the gym; then physical pain is a reality!). But when we think about what WE want to do—not what others want us to do—we should get revved up just by the thought of doing it.

Ambitious women understand that motivation is a key foundational driving force in their lives. In fact, a psychologist will tell you that motivation is the basic reason we do anything; it is the basis for all our behaviors.

After we moved to Texas, my husband opened a new contracting business, and I started working on a commission-only basis. Talk about motivation! But this is where I learned to sell, where I learned good people skills along with many other foundational principles I live by today.

What was my primary motivation? Our son, David, wanted to attend a private college in Oklahoma, and I wanted to pay the college tuition. I decided I would go for the biggest account I could in Tulsa and that would do two things: I could 1) travel to Tulsa more often to see him, and I could 2) make enough money to pay for his tuition. I worked really hard for months, made calls, did things I never thought I would do or could do, and eventually I got the account, the largest bank in Oklahoma, and the commission helped pay his tuition every year!

I believe that every experience we have in life is a stepping stone to something greater, and that should be motivation enough to keep moving forward in life. In my case, I had to start by getting the small, commission-only orders but that helped me get the big one!

Consider these ambitious and motivated women:

- • J.K. Rowling, the famous author of the Harry Potter series, was certainly motivated. Many a time, she has attributed her considerable achievements to her ability to focus all her attention on the things that mattered to her the most, the things that truly motivated her. Her storytelling abilities are a reminder that we can all be motivated by our gifts and talents.
- •A lady named Tererai Trent was raised in rural Zimbabwe and not allowed to go to school because she was female. Forced to marry a man at 13, she had three children by the time she was 18. Today, she has a doctorate degree from Western University because she believed in herself, and her dream of getting an education motivated her.

Did you see the movie *Saving Mr. Banks*? It is the true story about how the movie *Mary Poppins* came about. Walt Disney was so motivated to get Mrs. P.L. Travers to let him produce the story of Mary Poppins, he stopped at nothing. It took him 20 years to get the screen rights, but in 1961 *Mary Poppins* finally became a movie. Mr. Disney knew that *Mary Poppins* would be one of the biggest hits of all time, so he never let up. This movie is just one example of the Disney empire that we all know and love. Mr. Disney was, indeed, a motivated man!

Your Motivation

As an Ambitious Woman, I know you are motivated.

But do you know why? Where do you see yourself today? What about yesterday? Think about a time of family or personal crisis, or a time of great joy. How did you feel? What did you hope to accomplish? How did it affect you then, and how does it impact you today? Motivation involves meeting an unmet need and formulating a goal to do so.

When we are motivated, we want to be active and do things. We set goals, both short and long term, and move toward accomplishing them. There is often an element of pain in our desire to change; what we do or don't do affects us and those around us. So we make the determination of whether this goal, this desire, is strong enough to disrupt our lives and the lives of those around us.

It's been said that in order to be motivated to change things, you have to either have passion about something or be disturbed about something. Either one of these will drive you to be motivated.

Now that we understand more about *how* we are motivated, it's time to pull out our journals again and begin to reflect on *what* motivates us. Consider those times when you have looked forward to an event and how you felt in your body, mind, and spirit. Contrast those feelings with a time you were less than enthusiastic. What differences do you notice?

Allow me to offer a possibility. When you really wanted to do something, you felt excited, with no doubts and hesitation about what you were doing, whether it was preparing a business presentation or anticipating seeing your child after you'd been gone for a few days. But when you weren't thrilled—say you were scheduled for a root canal—you felt entirely different. You may have sighed, moaned to yourself, complained to others, and reluctantly dragged your feet to the appointment. You were motivated by pain relief, so you followed through, but you weren't thrilled about it.

Hopefully, you've begun to see how motivation is an integral part of your growth and journey through life. Motivation keeps us moving forward—I recognize that my goals are important and flexible as needed. We are each on our own life journey. We are all in different seasons of our lives, so different things will motivate us. Identifying how we are motivated helps us as we look forward.

Recognizing the significance of meeting unmet needs so we can become more whole and complete is a critical part of our motivation. Either we can look at this journey as drudgery, or we can face it with joy. Knowing my motivation makes the journey even more fun.

I am motivated to help and empower other women to reach their destiny. I could have never had an Ambitious Women's Conference or written an Ambitious Women's book if I was not motivated to do so.

What is your *Why?* What motivates you?

Write in your journal the things in life or business that will motivate you to accomplish great things!

BE MOTIVATED with YOUR WHY and it will help you be an Ambitious Woman!

Nancy Brinker is an Ambitious Woman. You can be one too.

LIVE A MOTIVATED LIFE!

Chapter 8

Live a Humble Life

Humility Underlines Success

One of the major attributes of an Ambitious Woman is her humility. Two of the most humble women I have had the privilege of knowing over the past several years are Lesley Chambless and Carolyn Thompson. Both have been incredible role models and encouragement to me.

Lesley's husband, Chris, was the 52nd employee of Excel Communications, a telecommunications company that sold long distance phone plans and exploded in the 90s. He eventually rose to the rank of vice president of marketing and acquired his wealth when the company went public.

Carolyn married Jere Thompson Jr., whose grandfather founded and started Southland Corporation, better known as 7-Eleven stores. Jere founded CapRock Communications, during the deregulation of long distance, selling it later for a hefty profit. In 2006, he and Chris founded a Texas retail electric provider, Ambit Energy, currently a billion dollar company with more than a million customers.

Despite their wealth and status, Lesley and Carolyn model humility. They are godly women who pray for their husbands and the companies they run, they stand behind them, they put their children first, and their priorities to family are evident. They are humble, Ambitious Women and they never forget where they came from. Their humility reminds me to never forget where I came from either. They remind me that humility is a hallmark of an Ambitious Woman.

But at close to the midpoint of this book, we are facing a dilemma. Every characteristic of an Ambitious Woman that we have previously discussed, and every characteristic that comes after this chapter, makes us feel good about ourselves and our accomplishments. How can we feel good and be humble at the same time?

I think you'll understand by the end of this chapter, so let's begin by asking yourself this question: "What does humble mean to me?" Go ahead and define it by writing down your definition in your journal. Remember, there's "the dictionary meaning" and then there's "what does humble mean to you?"

So did you write out your definition of humility? Humility is not easy to define or to live out, is it? Rick Warren says it best in his book *The Purpose Driven Life*: "Humility is not thinking less of yourself, it is thinking of yourself less."

Think about this: The opposite of humility is "pride," and not the kind of legitimate pride that comes from having accomplished goals. No, the kind of pride I'm talking about is the kind that lords it over other people and tries to make you look better at their expense. There's nothing wrong with being proud of what you've accomplished, but it's how you express that pride that makes the difference.

When we are humble, we don't go around telling everyone about our accomplishments. Humility tells you that you ARE special, and, because of that, your achievements will go before you. Rather than toot your own horn for the sake of praise or acknowledgement, let your accomplishments speak for you. Let others praise you; let your work speak for itself. You can continue to be uniquely you.

Defining Humility

If we want to understand the connection between humility and being an Ambitious Woman, let's look at some versions of the definition of humility. Merriam Webster says humility is "the quality or state of not thinking you are better than other people" and "the quality or state of being humble." *Webster's New World College Dictionary* states it is "the absence of pride or self-assertion" and also "the quality or state of being humble." A verse in the Bible puts it this way: "Do nothing from rivalry or conceit, but in humility count others more significant than yourselves. Let each of you look not only to his own interests, but also to the interests of others."

When you look at it that way, it means Ambitious Women *are* humble. Being humble means understanding our shortcomings; not being proud or self-assertive, but being modest. Ambition is going to get you a lot of what you want in life. And when successes pile up, you may start feeling pretty self-important. Humility, then, is your only hope of not getting "stuck" on yourself. Being humble will keep you grounded.

Back in chapter one, Diana Nyad said that although her accomplishments looked like a solitary effort, they really were a team effort. She could never have swum from Cuba without her team of about twenty-five people who helped her all along the way. In her victory, she was humble. When you realize that you cannot do it alone, that your success was really the efforts of others as well, you are humbled. If not, then you are prideful. You take all the credit.

Remember: NO ONE MAKES IT ALL ALONE!

A big part of being humble is not worrying about what I can't control. Humility includes knowing the limits of my abilities. I cannot do anything about many things that affect my life. While I can control my life, I cannot control someone else's—even if their life directly affects mine. I cannot control the government, but it can affect my life. I cannot control the weather, but it can certainly affect me. I cannot control people in your business, even though it may affect me and my finances.

Humility in Action

As an Ambitious Woman, it is better to develop humility rather than to be humbled forcibly by others or by circumstance. For example, what do you do if you were the team leader of a project at work or in your business? When the project is finished, and everyone is present, including management, do you take credit for the work others have done, or do you recognize and compliment those who made the project a success?

Humility requires that you know who you are; it requires that you treat people with love and respect. Humility and compassion go together. Humility, loyalty, and accountability are seen together in gracious Ambitious Women. Humility requires being positive and looking on the bright side. Doing so forces us to look outside ourselves and see the good in others and our circumstances. Being humble takes you out of the picture because it puts others first.

Maybe you feel you need to gain a sense of humility. If so, start helping people in need. You'll be amazed how grateful you are for your life, for who is in your life, and for the things you have. Then you'll be well on your way to living a humble life.

If you don't do so already, I challenge you to recognize the good in others. Recognize their achievements. In all things, put others first. Talk about them, not you. Invest your time in listening to others. Put yourself last and you will create a win-win.

Can you accept others unconditionally? That's not easy. When you're humble, you realize people won't live up to your expectations. They won't be able to fill all your needs. It's probably harder to accept those you know unconditionally than it is to accept strangers this way. This is something the Ambitious Woman continuously works on.

Humility goes the extra mile.

How do you manage to be humble when you're ambitious? How can you be humble when you're the boss or you are at the top of your game?

Humility means praising others for small achievements. Humility encourages. The truth is that the higher you go in leadership, in influencing others, and in affecting the lives of others, the more humility you will need.

Is there an area in your life where you need to put pride aside and be humble? Maybe you are perfect and you don't have any pride, but I highly doubt it. Think of at least one area where you can be a little bit more humble and write it down in your journal. Then begin to work on the character trait of being humble.

As I have attained success in my business, people tell me they want to be like me, they want to take pictures with me, or they want my autograph. I am so humbled and blown away by these requests. I never want money or fame to cause me to forget "where I came from." Remember, money can make you proud, and pride is the enemy of the successful and Ambitious Woman.

Remember these words: Never forget where you came from.

Lesley Chambless and Carolyn Thompson are Ambitious Women.

You can be one too. LIVE A HUMBLE LIFE!

Chapter 9

Live a Self-Disciplined Life

Discipline Is The Foundation Of Success

Sheryl Sandburg

Is there an Ambitious Woman more disciplined than Sheryl Sandburg, COO of Facebook? She is a role model for the modern woman! She is not only the number two person at Facebook, she is also the author of a best-selling book, *Lean In: Women, Work, and the Will to Lead.* She is also personal friends with the likes of Oprah, Bono, and Michael Bloomberg. With all the commitments and obligations she has in the corporate world, she is also a devoted wife and mother.[8]

Wow, how does she keep her life together? One word: D-I-S-C-I-P-L-I-N-E!

I once heard about an older woman who used to hit the tennis courts every morning from 6:30 to 7:15 a.m. Then it was a quick shower and to work by 8 a.m. One day, as she was hurrying to her car, she was asked why she was such a stickler

8 Excerpted from http://money.cnn.com/2013/10/10/leadership/sheryl-sandberg-mpw.pr.fortune/

for her schedule. Her answer was a good one: "If you don't have discipline, you don't have anything!"

Now that's a great answer.

The truth is that discipline is required if we want to get anywhere in life. It's the foundation of any success! Whether I'm talking to a member of my team, or speaking to an audience, I talk about being disciplined without actually saying, "YOU MUST BE DISCIPLINED!"

Instead, I try to give them an outline on which to build their business. My steps can be applied to any business and are inspired by Steven Covey's book, *7 Habits of High Effective People*. These steps help put discipline in place in order to achieve the success every Ambitious Woman wants.

1. *Begin With the End in Mind*
    - Set your goal. What do you want to do? What do you want to accomplish? (Be realistic—you may want to make a million dollars, but you aren't going to do that in a week.)
    - Reset your goal if you don't achieve it. (I call this: Disciplining your disappointments.)
2. *Help Your Team Set Goals (Synergize)*
    - Ask for commitment and accountability.
    - Commit to those who are your core group and pour into them.
3. *Know Your Numbers*

- Know what your financial freedom number is and how you will get it.

4. *Be Proactive*

- You must be a "think ahead" thinker and anticipate problems and solutions.

5. *Put First Things First*

- Faith, Family, Business.

6. *Think Win-Win*

- If you aren't in this to win, no one else will be.

7. *Seek First To Understand, Then To Be Understood*

- Success depends on communication, communication, and more communication.

8. *Sharpen the Saw*

- Know *every* aspect of what you are doing and determine that you will continue to grow by learning.

NEVER, EVER, EVER GIVE UP!

Following these steps takes discipline, but they are a blueprint for a successful endeavor.

From one Ambitious Woman to another, I encourage you to follow them.

*****

Pillars of Self-Discipline

The only thing harder than being disciplined enough to follow a path is to be *self-disciplined.* By definition, self- discipline is "the ability to control one's feelings and overcome one's weaknesses; the ability to pursue what one thinks is right despite temptations to abandon it." Self- discipline is tough. It grinds us. It tells us we need to get out of bed and get going when we would rather sleep in. It tells us to "stick with the plan." If we are going to accomplish anything, we need to live disciplined lives.

In order to reach the highest position in my company, I had to be incredibly self-disciplined. I had to give up a lot of things for a short season in order to accomplish my goals. After talking with my husband, we agreed that it would take a lot of hard work and sacrifices to get to the top. We made some one-time decisions that would pay off in the long run. For instance, I would be away from home several nights a week to do meetings. We would scale down our social life and give up TV and going to movies. We didn't even go on a real vacation for the first few years. When I look back on this period in my life, I see that I followed a plan that I now call the "three pillars of discipline." Here they are:

Pillar #1: Stick with it

No doubt you know people who start something and never finish it. The only thing worse than that is telling all your friends what you are doing and then not doing it. Accountability is supposed to help you to your goals and dreams, but it's a major let down if someone starts something and then doesn't finish it.

Discipline is sticking with something until it's done.

This "stick-to-it-iveness" is what enables women I know to set a goal that seems way out of their comfort zone … and several months later, they call me and say, "I did it!"

It's so awesome to see. Did they have the skill set first? Not at all! Had they done it before? Nope! Did they have all the answers when they started? Hardly!

What they had was a plan and the desire to stick with it until it was done.

It all comes back to discipline.

Pillar #2: Set your sights

Setting your goals is determining where you are going. That is a natural part of discipline, even though where you end up may be slightly different than where you previously imagined! That's the fun of goal-setting, but it's all part of the process of setting and achieving your goals.

Do you know what you want to do, accomplish, reach, attain? When you have that clarified, it's simply a matter of breaking down the individual steps that are necessary to get you there. Again, that is a role of discipline.

Discipline is the perfect meshing of your desire with your effort.

Your goals are the dreams and desires that rumble around in your heart and mind. They are there, waiting to come out. You know them, you breathe them, and you want desperately to live them. Discipline is what allows that to happen.

I believe that what you aim toward and pursue with passion must come to pass! It's simply unstoppable, and that's discipline at work. When you set out the steps necessary to reach your goals, it's just a matter of taking those steps and then … you will reach your goals!

Pillar #3: Choose it

At its core, discipline is a choice. It's up to you to choose it. Funny thing, and you know it, but you can't give or choose or "bless" someone else with discipline. They either apply it or they don't. It's up to them … and it's up to you.

When you set your mind to do something, and press continually toward it, you will achieve it. Discipline is that powerful!

Discipline and Habits

When it comes to reaching your own goals and dreams, and your desire to be an Ambitious Woman of influence, you're going to have to deal with the power your habits have on your life.

It's annoying that bad habits don't require any discipline to form. They are just there, right in front of us. From eating unhealthy food to thinking negative thoughts, the bad habits just seem so ready to form. They are like gravity almost: just there to affect you whether you like it or not!

Irritating, I know, but such is the case. Sadly, most people stop dealing with their bad habits, but they shouldn't! We can be and do anything we want, and getting these bad habits out of our way may be difficult … but it's certainly doable.

The answer? Yes, you've guessed it. It's discipline.

If you are not, by nature, a disciplined person, you can CHOOSE to be one. Once again, it all comes down to your choice. Do you want to be more focused, more positive, and accomplish what you've set out to do? Here are some easy choices you can make:

- VALUE your time!
- Limit wasted time watching television, playing computer games, or surfing the Web.
- Take time for reflection and/or meditation.
- Set goals for personal achievement and growth.
- Discipline your thought life.

What about you? You know what you want, and you know the good habits that need to form. Now take your journal out and write down the good habits that you need to work on.

Next, you will need to decide to apply discipline to make those habits a reality in your life. We all need to put discipline to work in our lives, though we all have different uses for that discipline. We all have ambitions. Here are a few disciplines that may help you get there even faster:

Remember the Passion

What is it that you do? Do you want to do it more, better, faster, stronger? Take a moment to go back to what made you do what you do. Was it the fun, the love, the community, or something else?

Whatever it was, reignite those dreams. We all easily forget things, so relive the stories, hear the passion again, and connect with what moved you, what caused you to be disciplined, in the first place.

If you are in sales, use the product or service again. Create a new story that compels you to take action with passion. Remember, stories are far more impactful than mere words, as they reflect passion. Get back to your passion and let it reignite the fire within you.

Discipline helps bring back the passion!

Choose to Improve

Is there something that you need to improve on, such as a selling skill or a personal relationship or a fitness habit? Whatever it is that you need to do, choose to improve. Set your sights to get better … and do it.

That's discipline.

If you want to be better on stage, speaking in front of people, then look for opportunities to do just that! Scary, yes, but it's going to make your goal come true. For instance, if you are in sales and the phone scares you, pick it up and start calling more sales prospects. I also suggest reading my all-time favorite book on the subject, *Carpe Phonum, How to Seize the Phone, Take Action and Call Your Prospects, Even When You Lack Courage:* by Tammy Stanley of "Sales Refinery." It will help you with discipline.

Always remember that discipline helps you IMPROVE.

Influence Others

If one of your goals is to positively influence more people, then you need to get out there and do exactly what you want to do. Discipline yourself to do just that. Look for ways to get in front of people, to give, and to help them toward their goals.

Influence is what leadership is all about, anyway, and you'll see that the more you positively influence others, the more people will be following you.

Discipline helps you influence more people.

A Disciplined Attitude

We all want an attitude that is disciplined. One way is to discipline your disappointments … yep, that is one of my favorite sayings! When you get a no or don't get the sale, contract, or job you want, that's where discipline comes in.

Remember the three pillars of discipline. They will help you to stay disciplined.

1) Stick to it

2) Set your sights

3) Choose it

When you have an attitude that will not be denied, *you* won't be denied, and that means you can overcome anything in your way. Discipline helps you maintain your killer attitude and "discipline those disappointments."

Financial Discipline

Are you looking to make more money? Discipline will help you get there faster than almost anything. I had to learn discipline in my outside sales job when I was given the quota of 20 cold calls a day. I remember there were days when it was almost 5:00 p.m. and I had only knocked on 18 doors. But my manager said I would not be successful unless I did 20. The quota was 20 cold calls every day. So either I could fudge and just do 18, or I could be disciplined and knock on all 20 doors. Discipline helped me press on to do the quotas, which led to being a top producer.

The Ambitious Woman knows that discipline helps her make more money.

It Ain't Luck

Some people seem lucky, don't they? They are working

on an idea, and then it turns into something else, and before you know it, eBay, Google, Yahoo, and Facebook are born!

"She's just lucky," people say, but don't you believe it.

The truth is that luck happens when preparation and opportunity meet up. Did you catch that? It's the person who is preparing, working, planning, and being all-around disciplined who gets hit with the opportunity that makes other people salivate.

Consider a woman I know who seemingly struck it rich. She is making well over six figures, and an outsider might think she inherited it or was given it in a divorce settlement, or flat out can't imagine how she did it. The truth is that every penny has come from her own efforts. She started a business, learned the ropes, and applied herself. She went out and made the sales calls, she drove in the rain, she missed the TV shows that other people were watching, and now she's enjoying the results of her efforts.

If you call her lucky, she'd probably slap you. It ain't luck at all. It's discipline, sure and consistent discipline, coupled with a business that brings profits.

You can be that woman!

Discipline applies to all of us, no matter what we are doing. Discipline will prepare you for opportunity to strike, and when it does, you'll be ready!

Conclusion

You are in an amazing place in your life this very moment. You really are. You are an incredible person, and you have what it takes to get you to the next level. On top of that, you know where you are going. You are on your way!

I'm excited for you. I really am, and that excitement isn't based on hype or pipe dreams. Not at all! Discipline is the foundation of any great success, and discipline is at work in your life.

There is no limit to this either. I mean, discipline is here for the taking. We can all take all we want and apply it to every area of life. Amazingly, we can apply it right now

… and it will bring good results!

It's an exciting time, so go out and be disciplined.

Sheryl Sandburg is an Ambitious Woman. You can be one too.

LIVE A DISCIPLINED LIFE!

Chapter 10

Live a Loyal Life

Loyalty—The Sometimes Forgotten Virtue

One of the greatest examples of loyalty between women is found in the Bible. In the book of Ruth, we find an incredible story of a mother and daughter-in-law. In this book, Naomi travels to Moab with her husband and sons, because there is a great famine in the nation of Israel. Soon after, her husband dies. Then after 10 years, both her sons die, leaving Naomi alone with her daughters-in-law. When she hears that God has blessed Israel with crops, she decides to leave Moab and return to Israel. She then encourages both of her daughters-in-law to stay in Moab and remarry. One of them decides to do so. However, Ruth says to Naomi, "Don't ask me to leave you! Let me go with you. Wherever you go, I will go; wherever you live I will live. Your people will be my people, your God will be my God" (Wow, can you believe that? Most people would have been focused on their own lives. Forget Naomi—she's old! I need to take care of myself!).

It is a story of real loyalty.

Naomi and Ruth then travel to Israel, where they are welcomed back by the villagers in her hometown of Bethlehem. It is now harvest time and, after they have settled down in Naomi's house, Ruth goes out into the fields to gather grain for the coming winter. Now comes the best part—a true love story develops! Boaz, a relative of Naomi's, sees Ruth gathering grain, and he becomes intrigued by her. Later that evening, he invites her to dinner to find out more about her. When he sees how beautiful she is, and hears of her loyalty to Naomi, he falls in love … and the rest is history! They marry and have children and live happily ever after.

Ruth's loyalty paid off.

There are so many things in life that demand loyalty from us: relationships, products, employers, restaurants. Companies build large-scale marketing campaigns around their brand to develop loyalty within their customers. As women, sometimes loyalty makes us choose one item over the other even if the one is on sale.

Loyalty is important but, sadly, it has almost disappeared in our society. Think about the skyrocketing divorce rate. Or the constant movement from job to job. Volunteer organizations only have a few loyal members.

The truth is that through technology and innovation, the world has changed. We are now much more loyal to ourselves than we have ever been. As women, we need connection; we need and thrive on loyalty, whether at home, at work, or in our friendships. That's one of the reasons I started *The Ambitious Women's Conference*. Women can come together with one purpose, one goal—to connect, network, and share successes and even failures.

Women love to be together. We learn and grow differently than men. We build our businesses differently than men. We make long-lasting, loyal friends. My friend Tina is a great example; she has been with me from the planning stages of the conference. She has been loyal as the executive director, and I could not host the conference without her.

Without loyalty—our loyalty to others and their loyalty to us—we cannot truly feel complete.

I think loyalty has become somewhat of a lost virtue. But then something happens that reminds me what loyalty is all about. I have a friend, Kathy, whom I have known since my days of living in San Diego. A few years back, we reconnected in Corpus Christi, where she had moved, and now I try to see her every time I'm there. I knew we were really good friends, but I did not consider what a loyal friend she was until after the following occurred.

I was trying to get on a flight back home from Corpus Christi, because I had engagements I needed to be at the next two days. Kathy was going to take me and my sister to the airport. However, during lunch, the weather turned bad and we kept getting texts that the flight had been delayed, then another text, and another … then the dreaded words: CANCELED! We would not be able to get out until 9:00 p.m. the next evening. By that time, I would have missed both engagements.

We sat there contemplating what to do. Rent a car? Go to San Antonio and catch a flight? Wait until Friday night? It was inevitable; no matter what, I would miss that night's engagement, but I could NOT miss Friday night. As I sat there, unmistakably disturbed, Kathy piped up. "Well, I'm not doing anything; I'll just drive you home."

"What? Tonight?" I replied. "That's a seven hour drive. And then what?"

"I'll just drive back home," she said.

And that is what she did. She drove my sister and me to Fort Worth, Texas, seven hours straight, without a bag, toothbrush, or change of clothes.

Now that is an ambitious, loyal friend who gave with no regard to herself. I consider myself loyal, but I'm not even sure I would do that. At least not without complaining.

Loyalty is truly a trait needed for the Ambitious Woman.

Loyalty to Yourself

Being loyal to yourself is about being dedicated to the things that interest you, support you, and push you forward. Sometimes our needs get lost in the shuffle of life. The people we love can dominate our lives, and we can begin serving and doing things for them but neglecting our very own needs. As women, it is important that we take care of our physical bodies, mental health, and emotional well- being. It is time that we become loyal to ourselves.

After all, we are going to be with ourselves for the rest of our lives.

So, first, you need to be loyal to yourself.

Let's start with your belief system: It's key to the ability to be loyal to yourself.

Loyalty to self requires knowing what you believe. Loyalty to yourself is neither selfishness nor self- centeredness. Loyalty to yourself is NOT "looking out for No. 1." Loyalty to yourself is founded in what you stand for. What do you believe in, what do you call truth? This is your lighthouse, your guide. Are you being true to what you believe?

When you don't know what you believe in, you're standing on shifting sand. As the sand erodes from under your feet, you'll have to shift as well. Being true to your beliefs means knowing what you believe. This puts you on solid ground that won't erode beneath you. What's more, you can move around on it if you want because it is solid beneath your feet. Knowing your values is key to being loyal to yourself.

Loyalty requires discipline and time. You do not develop loyalty to yourself overnight. Above all, loyalty asks you to love yourself enough to be faithful to who you are. It requires that you prioritize the things that matter most to you. Maybe you are not loyal to yourself. Maybe you are putting others first in your life and resenting that you don't have enough "me time." Remember: Being loyal—even to yourself—takes time.

First things first. Draw up two lists. Your first list should be about the things you want to do or that you need to do for yourself. For example, your list might read: read one book a month, physical activity three times a week, put aside $50 for spending money, sign up for cooking classes or dance classes.

Then create a second list for all the things you do for others. Don't forget the small stuff!

If you care for your parents or volunteer at a local non-profit, include that in there as well. Then put those lists side by side. Your challenge is to create a third list that is to be placed directly in the center of those two lists. This new list should incorporate your "you items" as well as items on the "others list." This list is not for you to resent all that you do for others, but to provide you a realistic view of where your priorities are.

The most important point is that you must come first in your life. You have yourself at the end of the day and must be happy with all that you are, your accomplishments, your future, and your present. I learned a long time ago and have shared with many unhappy people that your happiness cannot depend on anyone else—not your husband, your friends, or even your business. Happiness depends on YOU.

Why is this so important? Because if you are burned out from meeting the needs of others, you will grow resentful and bitter; you'll be no good to anyone. While some people think that putting their own needs above the needs of others is selfish, nothing could be further from the truth. Women are relationship driven, so we naturally want to take care of others. Here is a truth: If you are no good to yourself, you are no good to others.

Loyalty and Change

As women, things are always changing in our lives. Our bodies are changing (something none of us like), our tastes and preferences are changing, and sometimes the things we love change. Change is so important to our lives because without it we do not grow and mature.

Have you ever met a person who does not appreciate change? Sit back for a moment and look at her life. Do they look or even sound happy? Chances are she probably does not. It is difficult to oppose change and still maintain a lasting happiness. Just like any relationship, people change. The ability to change and grow with someone else, whether in a marriage or a friendship, is one of the most difficult changes to be loyal to. That person could be changing into someone maybe you do not care for any longer. As you grow and change so are the people, relationships, and things around you.

Be in tune with change. Know the difference between a change for the good and a change for the worse. Be in tune to yourself and embrace the change that you will go through. It is healthy to grow and change. Most importantly, be okay with changing your preferences, tastes, likes, and dislikes. Be loyal to the changes in your life, and you will be a loyal person.

Being Loyal

I have many other people who are loyal to me, and I to them. I think of Paula, because she introduced my husband and me. She has remained a loyal and faithful friend to both of us all these years. I always told her if anything happened to us, she is responsible for our four children.

There are Angela and Suzie, whom I met while we were all young marrieds and had babies at the same time. Sometimes we'd be separated for years due to circumstances and moves, but we always remained loyal friends. Our children have known each other since birth, and even now my sons, Aaron and David, and their sons, Chris and Nathan, remain loyal friends. They live in separate states but still are staying in contact and sharing their own children now.

Then there is Billy and Linda. Only loyal friends would drive your moving truck clear across the country with your most treasured possessions, four children, a grandmother, a cat and dog, a pickup truck with a washer and dryer, and a surfboard. Well, they did, and later on they ended up moving themselves to Texas and raising their children there as well.

That's loyalty.

I also have a friend I have known longer than any other friend. We met when I was just 18, and we have been through everything together—jobs, marriages, divorces, births of children, loss of children, deaths of parents, good times, bad times … you name it, we've been through it together. Most recently, my dear friend called me to tell me that she was diagnosed with Stage IV Non-Hodgkin's lymphoma cancer. I could not believe it. Not my friend Nancy! She is the one person who loves life so much, loves who she is, she loves dancing, she loves beer, and she loves everyone and everything around her. It should never happen to a person like that!

I was at the airport getting ready to board a plane when Nancy called me, crying. But I took a moment and prayed with her on the phone, right then and there in the airport, with everyone boarding. I wanted to be a loyal friend, and so as soon as I could, I flew out to spend several days with her in Palm Springs, where we had some precious and fun times cherishing our friendship. While there, I asked if she would share with me her thoughts on loyalty. Here is what she recently sent me:

Webster's definition of loyalty is being true and faithful … keeping promises and being obedient to duty and commitment. It is being true and constant always. I am proud to say that I have remained loyal throughout my life.

I have always been a loyal parent to my daughter Mariah, making a commitment to never date after my divorce until she was out of high school. I have been a loyal employee to General Electric for forty years and a very loyal friend to many. Some of my still active and constant friendships go back as far as grade school and high school. In my extended family support group, our friendships began over thirty years ago and are still stronger than ever today!

In spite of my recent diagnosis of cancer I have been loyal by still working my side business from a hospital bed or Infusion Center while receiving chemotherapy treatment.

Above all and foremost, I have been loyal to my Creator, God the Father Almighty, who helps me face life's challenges head on with strength, courage, faith, hope, and grace.

Wow! I think she really understands what being loyal is! Although she has been dealt a bad card in life, she does not blame anyone, and she does not become disloyal to her job, her business, her friends, or God.

Some women feel they have no reason to be loyal. Trust has been shattered from childhood trauma, betrayal, or broken relationships. Their confidence is at an all-time low. But loyalty isn't about the other person—it's about you. And you can decide whom to be loyal to.

Here are some things to think about when you are working on being loyal:

Be supportive. Whether it is a friend or a spouse, we are supportive of others, not because we will get something back, but because we want to instill a sense of confidence, significance, and security in the other person.

Be upfront. I hate gossip, and I'm sure you do too. But we must ask ourselves: Am I the source of the gossip? Loyalty means we don't gossip, we don't back-stab, and we don't start rumors.

Be honest. Loyalty means you are honest with your thoughts and feelings. Don't just say what others want to hear; that makes you wimpy, a YES person, not a loyal person. Give your opinion and back it up with reasons. At the same time, be wise when you are honest. Telling your friend her outfit isn't as flattering as it could be might be acceptable. But telling her she looks like death warmed over is sure to offend.

Be balanced. It is easy to find yourself caught between being loyal to two different things or different people. Being loyal to one means being disloyal to the other. Instead of picking sides, be fair, open, and honest. While some people won't like this approach, it is best to avoid choosing sides, unless this is something you must obviously do.

Be willing to apologize. Loyalty doesn't mean you are perfect. If you have made a mistake, said the wrong thing, or done the wrong thing, do your best to amend the situation. Apologize. Correct the mistake, and learn from it.

As an Ambitious Woman, I implore you to be loyal—to your spouse, your family, your friends, your church—and especially to yourself! Loyalty will pay you benefits far beyond monetary gain.

Make a decision today to be loyal in good times and bad, happy times and sad. When you look back over your life, being loyal is something you'll always be proud of.

Who are your loyal friends, and whom can you be loyal to? Think about it and write it down in your journal. When you look back over your life, you'll always be proud that YOU ARE LOYAL.

My friend Nancy is an Ambitious Woman. You can be one too.

LIVE A LOYAL LIFE!

Chapter 11

Live a Persistent Life

Quitters Never Succeed

Jacqueline Kennedy Onassis

I remember watching President John Kennedy's funeral as a young girl. While I didn't understand the impact his death had on our nation, I was mesmerized by Jackie Kennedy. I was in awe of the strength she exhibited and the heartache she had to endure. Can you imagine riding in a motorcade, waving to the crowd one moment, and then watching your husband get shot the next?

Jacqueline Kennedy became the First Lady at the age of 31. Despite her world-fame, one of her major priorities was to be a good mother. She told a reporter that "if you bungle raising your children, I don't think whatever else you do well matters very much."

Five years after John F. Kennedy's death, this Ambitious Woman married Greek shipping magnate Aristotle Onassis. After his death, she persisted and went to work as an editor in New York City. She died on May 19, 1994, at the age of 64.[9]

*****

All of us have days when things look bleak, when it's hard to find the energy to persevere. But being persistent may determine our chances of success more than any other single characteristic.

Some parents wish their children were less persistent, especially during the toddler years. When Samson, my grandson was 4 years old, he was one of those toddlers and still remains persistent in everything he does. I can't help but indulge him every time he comes over and persistently asks for a Popsicle until his "meme" finally gives him one. But persistence is a wonderful trait in a human being. It's essential to accomplishing what you want in life. I'm sure when Samson develops this trait in the right direction, there is nothing he won't accomplish.

If you study Nobel Prize winners, they all have unique stories. But they share one thing: The people who know them always describe how that person never gave up. A two-year scientific experiment can fizzle, and that scientist will be back in the lab the next morning, figuring out what she can learn from whatever went wrong.[9]

Steve Jobs, at 30, was left devastated and depressed after being unceremoniously removed from the company he started. Oprah Winfrey was demoted from her job as news anchor because she "wasn't fit for television." Malcolm Forbes, once publisher of *Forbes Magazine*, one of the largest

9 Excerpted from http://www.jfklibrary.org/JFK/Life-of-Jacqueline-B- Kennedy.aspx

business publications in the world, did not make the staff of his school newspaper at Princeton University. So what happened here? What made these famous failures into the wildly successful people they ultimately became?

The solution to a crisis or a problem may not be easy to discover. However, a winner will relentlessly pursue new avenues and consistently experiment. In the final analysis, success may only be a matter of persistence.

Persistence is not taught, it is modeled. Some people in their lives showed that these "failures" or setbacks are only temporary. We as parents, teachers, managers, and entrepreneurs must continuously demonstrate the need for beginning a difficult task, for hanging in there, and following through. This may be the most important attribute we teach.

Yes You Can

As an Ambitious Woman, you CAN develop the quality of persistence. By picking yourself up when you fall, over and over if necessary, you can keep pushing yourself onward. Remember, success is just around the corner.

One summer we decided it was time that Luke, also another four-year-old grandson at the time, learned to swim, and we signed him up for swimming lessons. On the first day, he reluctantly went, crying. He believed he would sink to the bottom of the pool without his little shark floatie. But he daily persisted, trying to swim without his sharkie. The second day, the third day, the fourth day, and finally on the seventh day he actually kicked, moved his arms, and swam several feet. He was so excited. He could actually float without his sharkie! He learned persistence, even though it was hard at first. This trait, developed in the right direction, will give him limitless opportunities.

We couldn't teach Luke to be persistent. He learned it from watching his older sister and the other children in class, so he kept trying. Persistence paid off; he can now swim like a fish!

The greatest challenges you will have in life occur when the going gets tough. Many entrepreneurs start to believe what others say and allow negativity to creep in when things get tough. However, both the greatest challenges and the toughest times build character. Battling through adversity and rebuilding from disappointment builds the habit of persistence. Persistence builds strength of character and develops self-discipline. It is this mentality that is built over a period of time that will carry you forward through any obstacle that life will throw at you.

When people see a successful person they often associate her success with luck or being in the right place at the right time. They rarely see all the many small failures and obstacles they faced week after week for years until they eventually made it. I once read a quote from the great actress, Julie Andrews, who said: "Perseverance is failing 19 times and succeeding the 20th." That is so true.

Your greatest asset in business (and life) is your ability to do one task and stick to it until it is complete. Finish the race and finish strong! Don't stop midway. The prize goes to those who persist and finish! Many great minds have said through the years that it is adversity that makes the man. I think that adversity also makes the Woman!

As an Ambitious Woman, persistence is extremely important! It will help you know what you want in life and help you to focus on achieving it. Persistence will help you focus on the "long term" without losing sight of the day-to- day. It will help you in your quest for wisdom, achievement, success, fulfillment, and self-confidence.

I'm sure you know people who are persistent. I encourage you to LEARN FROM THESE PEOPLE and become a persistent person yourself so that others can learn from you. Persistence involves setting goals, committing to a course of action, making the necessary sacrifices, overcoming obstacles, setbacks, and criticism—all the while maintaining your motivation, energy, and faith. It requires adaptability and flexibility as you maintain a path of creative action to accomplish your goals. Persistence can reenergize you when you go through the inevitable "down" days.

As an Ambitious Woman, you know that persistence is key to doing anything worthwhile in life. Some people might tell you that you should never set your goals too high if you have only a minimum of talent or education. However, how do you think successful people got to where they are? With persistence! Anyone who has succeeded in reaching their goals will tell you it takes hard work—a lot of hard work. Many will tell you why you shouldn't bother expecting big results if you have no natural talent. People with natural ability work hard to develop the skills they are known for. We only see the results of their efforts.

Always remember this: Quitting is only a decision away.

Even if it's something that you truly love, the option to quit is always there, tempting you. "Go on, stay in bed. What's a few wasted hours going to hurt? It's just too hard. You will never do it." Have you heard such words, or similar ones, going through your head? That's the voice of "the quitter," as I call it, talking to you. But the voice of persistence says, "You CAN do it." You might not always be motivated, you might not always have a good mindset, and you even might want to quit. But deciding to be persistent—and it is a decision you make—will always keep you going.

Here is a truth: When you feel most frustrated, when you feel like a failure, when the overwhelming desire to give up consumes you, your decision to be persistent will carry you through.

Prepare to Take Steps

I'm sure you realize by now that persistence makes a fundamental difference between success and permanent failure. As an Ambitious Woman, you need to develop, and redevelop continually, the vital quality of persistence. Here are some great steps to take.

- Decide what you want to accomplish and set goals. We all know how important setting goals is for achieving success, so take some time to figure out what it is you want. Do you want to lose ten pounds, graduate from college, run a marathon, or be a business success? A study I read several years ago showed that people who set clear, concise goals succeeded in achieving them 95% of the time! The common trait in all people who met their goals was a decision they made to refuse to quit and walk away.

- Prepare for obstacles and setbacks. You know that no one gets a free pass in life. My granddaughter Kate loves to play the game of Monopoly with her great grandmother, who is 91 at the time of this writing. Her goal is to always pass GO and collect $200. But you know what? Sometimes, you get the "Go to Jail" card instead. She does not get a free pass unless she persists and keeps drawing until she draws the "Get Out Of Jail Free" card. And she is developing her persistent trait by never finishing until she wins the game.

The fact is that troubles are going to come. People are going to upset you. Roadblocks will be set up to stop you cold in your tracks. Acknowledge these facts, but don't let them stop you. Instead, prepare for them. Nothing good was ever accomplished without overcoming adversity. Know and accept that there will be obstacles and setbacks; then prepare for them. Nothing important was ever accomplished without adversity, setbacks, and difficulties to contend with along the way.

Have you heard of Bethany Hamilton, the young surfer from Hawaii who had her left arm bitten off by a shark? She started surfing when she was just a child. At age 13, an almost-deadly shark attack resulted in her losing her left arm. She was back on her surfboard one month later and, two years after that, she won first place in the Explorer Women's Division of the NSSA National Championships. Talk about being persistent!

Maybe you didn't know this about Oprah Winfrey. She was repeatedly molested by a cousin, an uncle, and a family friend. At age 14, she gave birth to and lost a child. But she didn't let her tragic early life stop her. She became an honors student in high school and won an oratory contest that earned her a full scholarship to college. Today, she has millions of admirers and a net worth of almost $3 billion!

Here are some things you can do to develop persistence in your life:

- Take the first step. You cannot persevere, much less succeed, if you never try. Procrastination, fear of failure, and low self-esteem will all keep you frozen in your tracks. You won't fail if you never try. However, you will never succeed either. As the popular saying goes, "The only real failure in life is the failure to try."

- Review, reevaluate, and revise. If things do not work out the way you hoped, then simply go back and review your process. What went wrong? What didn't work? Where did it go wrong? (Notice I said "it" not "you." This simple change of words takes away the inevitable guilt and condemnation.) Ambitious Women know to revise and improve so they can move forward.

- Get support and encouragement. Stay away from naysayers and find people who will encourage and support you and give you honest, objective feedback. Ask them for advice, suggestions, and recommendations—and be humble enough to listen and receive from them.

- Maintain focus. I am a big fan of visualization. When you can "see" yourself obtaining your goal, you will keep "your eye on the prize." Make a vision board, and then begin to see yourself with or doing everything on that board. Write encouraging quotes. Put them on your mirror, in your closet, in your car, on your computer, in your journal, everywhere. They will help you stay persistent. Here are a few of my favorites.

"One mistake does not have to rule a person's entire life."

– Joyce Meyer

"We are made to persist. That's how we find out who we are."

– Tobias Wolff

"Success doesn't come to you; you go to it."

– T. Scott McLeod

"To persist with a goal, you must treasure the dream more than the costs of sacrifice to attain it."

– Richelle E. Goodrich

"Persistence and determination are always rewarded."

– Christine Ricelossians

"Let us not become weary in doing good, for at the proper time we will reap a harvest if we do not give up."

– (Galatians 6:9)

"Life is short, fragile and does not wait for anyone. There will NEVER be a perfect time to pursue your dream and goals."

– Unknown

"Champions keep playing until they get it right."

– Billie Jean King

"It does not matter how slowly you go as long as you do NOT stop."

– Confucius

"If you set out to be liked, you would be prepared to compromise on anything at any time, and you would achieve nothing."

– Margaret Thatcher

> "You may encounter many defeats, but you must not be defeated. In fact, it may be necessary to encounter the defeats, so you can know who you are, what you can rise from, how you can still come out of it."
>
> **– Maya Angelou**

> "Women must try to do things as men have tried. When they fail, their failure must be a challenge to others."
>
> **– Amelia Earhart**

BE PERSISTENT! It will help you be the Ambitious Woman you desire to be.

Jacqueline Kennedy Onassis was an Ambitious Woman.

You can be one too.

LIVE A PERSISTENT LIFE!

Chapter 12

Live a Consistent Life

Live Your Values Every Day

My friend Rainey Matthews is the perfect model of consistency. She is now 65 years *young*, yet was diagnosed with a "medical mystery" at age 53. She suffered trauma to her neurological system that resulted in severe mental and physical disability. Yet her condition did not diminish her mindset or her zest for life. She has always had compassion for the disabled, but now her new state in life has heightened her desire to see the needs of the disabled met on every level.

After she was told that she would never work again and that she would spend her life confined to a wheelchair, she defiantly said, "It was not a matter of proving the doctors wrong; it is a matter of having CONSISTENT determination to *not* have to live with these life sentences."

Today, Miss Rainey, as we all respectfully call her, is still an active participant in life. She is involved in her church, intercessory prayer groups, networking groups, and Foreign Accent Support systems. She is involved in various women's ministries, conducts individual and group mentoring, and hosts Bible study groups, all while working a part time business to achieve financial freedom.

Miss Rainey continues to have very lofty but achievable, goals for the future. She wants to support Southern California Teen Challenge and to become founder of the "Balm of Healing Haven Resort for Women," a place for women to go who are "emotionally hidden" while living public lives. She also wants to develop and expand "EMOTIONS by Design," a writing business enterprise she started in 2004.

*****

Consistency means "always acting or behaving in the same way. It is doing the same thing over and over in the same way." If you want to be ambitious, if you want to be successful, being consistent in whatever you choose to do is crucial to your success. *Little Things Matter*, by W. Todd Smith, is a great book to read. It has 100 ways to improve your life by doing the "little things" and doing them better and with greater consistency.

The Ambitious Woman, however, is consistent in more than just her actions; she is consistent in her attitudes, thoughts, and lifestyle. There are certain things you'll have to do every day. These are actions. For example, Miss Rainey always looks fabulous. Every time you see her she is dressed to the hilt—matching hat, jewelry, shoes, outfit, all color-coordinated. I always look to see what she's wearing. She is my "soul sista" in style. She is one of my heroes, and I cannot imagine living her life with the grace, patience, and consistency that she exhibits. As well as actions, there are certain things you live by. These are your values. You must be consistent in both areas. Consistency in your daily activities, in striving to meet your goals, is a matter of committing to doing what you have to do. Consistency in your values, meanwhile, is a matter of knowing who you are and what you believe in.

Being consistent takes work, at least at first. This is real work—you'll have to muster your motivation, your vision, and determination. It is said that it takes 30 days to form a habit—consistency is a good habit—and a habit is something we do consistently. One of my leadership mentors, John Maxwell, puts it this way: "It doesn't matter how talented you are. It doesn't matter how many opportunities you receive. If you want to grow, consistency is key."

You have to train yourself to be consistent, and you do this by starting small. You'll work your way up in achievements by committing to an easily attained goal.

My Perspective

Writing this book is an example of being consistent. When I started, I was apprehensive. I've spoken in front of thousands of people. I write a blog and do interviews, but bringing my thoughts into book form was challenging. I didn't think I would be able to do it. There were just not enough hours in a day. There are so many things to do, places to go, people to see. I knew I would never have hours on end in one big block or time frame, so I set a goal I could achieve: I determined to write for 15 minutes a day, no matter what.

And I was consistent. I found time every day to sit and write, even if only a few words came out.

I want you to know, this wasn't easy! I didn't want to do it, but I committed myself to doing it. As you can see, it worked. Not only did I sit each day in front of the computer and try to write, but I got better at it. I got to the point that I looked forward to the writing, especially as momentum began to show a result. The result? Now I'm an author because I was consistent; because I sat down to write every day, no matter what.

You won't succeed if you don't apply your efforts, consistently, to doing what you don't like doing. You must make up your mind to do what must be done.

Most people don't know this about me, but I was a surfer girl. Yes, I grew up on the beaches of southern California, and I started learning to surf when I was in high school. I had a friend nicknamed "Insect" who taught me. Surfing was one of the hardest things I attempted, at first. But by applying consistent effort every day, I became pretty good. Even after not surfing for 30 years, I was able to pick it back up on a trip to Costa Rica one year. I was quite impressed with myself but it all came down to the consistent work I did 30 years earlier.

So, how do you get consistency? At least three things are required:

1. You have to be motivated by your vision.

2. You have to know what you stand for.

3. You have to just bite the bullet and do it.

Consistent Purpose

Doing what needs to be done is easier if you know why you're doing it. Have you heard the phrase, "Know your WHY"? Knowing your why will help you stay consistent.

Brenda Lange is a woman who knows her Why. In 1993, she founded Orphans Unlimited, and she has built two orphanages, a medical clinic, and a malnutrition clinic, in Mozambique, Africa. In 1996, she built the Village of Love (VOL), and the Bread of Life Children's Center was founded in 2000, which has rescued over 500 orphaned, abandoned, and malnourished kids per year. Government officials have proclaimed her program as a "model that other organizations should copy."

Like Brenda, you have to know what you believe in, what you stand for, and what you want out of life. You have to know your purpose. Your purpose will be your compass and your guide. You can always look to your purpose and get your bearings."[10]

In *The Purpose Driven Life*, Rick Warren says consistently following your "compass" will keep you moving in the right direction. Are you unable to figure out what must be done? Look to your beliefs. What's right? What's truth? What's your purpose in life, and what are your dreams and vision?

Here's another meaning of consistency: "Showing

10 For more information go to: http://www.orphansunlimited.org/

steady conformity to character, profession, belief, or custom." Consistency isn't just setting goals and doing them every day. Consistency isn't just forming habits. It's conforming—being true—to what you believe.

Be absolutely sure what you believe in. If you're not sure, take time to meditate on it, to study, to seek a mentor's input. Your beliefs may change, but don't let them "fade." When the consistency of your moral foundation crumbles, you'll lose your motivation, your "why," and you're at risk of losing your momentum. Without the motivation that comes from your belief system, you'll stop acting.

Be consistent in your beliefs. Consistent in your morals. Consistent in integrity. Your truth will change sometimes—don't be afraid to look inward when you're not sure something you believe in is true for you anymore.

You've got to develop and decide who you are.

Consistent Actions

Let's talk more about consistency in your actions.

You must become self-motivated. You have to retain some excitement about your dreams and vision.

Ambitious Women aren't naturally idle. They want to achieve. They know the things that you have to do every day, and they can usually get up and go at it.

John Maxwell has a Rule of Five that he teaches in order to have consistency in your life. It is the five things that you should do every day. By doing them, you will develop consistency. Everyone's Rule of Five can be different, but these are the five things I try to do every day: read, write, pray, encourage, and add people to my circle of relationships. As a result of doing this for the past several years, I'm better educated, I'm a better writer, I'm more in touch with God, and I have a growing business and more meaningful relationships.

Consistency starts with commitment. Enlist your accountability partner to help you become consistent. There will come a point that your efforts become natural to you and, at that point, you just stay with it.

But being consistent isn't necessarily simply doing the same thing every day, or every weekday, or on a set schedule. It's not being a robot. Part of consistency is keeping the right perspective: circumstance, situation, who you are, and how they all gel together.

To achieve your dreams, you have to get outside your comfort zone. Remember, most people don't start at the top. I didn't get to start at the top in my business. I had to start at the bottom and consistently do all the things that I did not want to do! That's how I got to the top. Period!

Know your purpose and your principles.

Set small, achievable goals and attend to them daily. Write down a list of the things you need to do daily, weekly, and even hourly, to achieve your ambition. Start with the hardest one, and begin with little, easily accomplished steps. I promise you it won't be the hardest forever. Determine what your Rule of Five is, write it down, and start to be consistent with doing them every day.

Before you know it, you'll BE CONSISTENT! Rainey Matthews is an Ambitious Woman.

You can be one too.

LIVE A CONSISTENT LIFE!

Chapter 13

Live a Passionate Life

Passion Will Take You Anywhere You Want To Go

Barbara Walters

I love talk show hosts, and I love newscasters. I love to watch how they talk, look, and react. I love everything about the profession. If I could have chosen anything I wanted to be in life, I may have chosen to be one! I don't know of anyone in television with more passion, more zeal, more get-up-and-go than Barbara Walters. I watched her 20/20 program religiously for years. She retired after almost 5 decades in the profession, traveling around the world in search of the best news and human interest stories. I watched her final goodbye interview on *The View* and yes, I have to admit, I was moved to a few tears, which is not in my nature.

I am particularly impressed by her quote: "A woman can do anything. She can be traditionally feminine and that's all right; she can work, she can stay at home; she can be aggressive; she can be passive; she can be any way she wants with a man. But whenever there are the kinds of choices there are today, unless you have some solid base, life can be frightening."[11]

What a passionate woman! What an Ambitious Woman!

*****

I'm sure you have had many dreams of what you want to be and who you want to be. But have you ever had a dream that got you so excited that upon waking, you wish you could go back to sleep and relive it? I dreamed once that I was in the mountains hiking (which I don't even like to do) and I stumbled upon a big cave that was full of shoes! I walked into the cave and was in there for hours trying on thousands of pairs of shoes. It was so real I never wanted to leave the cave. But alas, I woke up and stumbled in my little closet with only my own pairs of shoes! It was quite a rude awakening. Especially since beautiful shoes are one of my passions.

Have you ever thought of how life would be if you had unlimited time, freedom, or resources? What would you do? What impact would you have on your family or community? Or how about this: Think of a time in your life where you felt the most satisfied. What were you doing? Were you helping someone, teaching someone, singing, dancing, writing, surfing? Now think of another time. What were you doing? What were you thinking or feeling? Relive that moment in

11 http://thinkexist.com/quotes/barbara_walters/

your mind. Feel that emotion. What fueled that emotion? It was your PASSION.

Passion is strong. Compelling. Fulfilling. It consumes you. It takes over you. It drives you. Your passion is a great indicator of your purpose in life. Without it, life seems mundane and fruitless. Day-to-day activities have less enjoyment; and the nagging question of, "Is there something else I should be doing?" never seems to be answered. With passion, you have a reason to rise up early and go to bed late. You have a sense of direction to follow.

We all have something that is unique about us. Something that sets us apart from the rest of the crowd. A talent, an ability, a calling. It is your creative mark you can leave upon the world.

I absolutely love to read stories about women with passion. Recently, I came across a profile of Shauna Miller, founder of Pennychic. In case you don't know, Shauna Miller is a Los Angeles-based fashionista, entrepreneur, designer, author, and the founder of Penny Chic, a fashion blog featuring looks styled from discount stores within 15 miles of every home in America. She knew that everyone wanted to look good but could not always afford it. I love to go through her website because I've always believed that when you go shopping you don't have to spend a lot of money on something; it just has to look like it costs a lot of money!

Here is an excerpt from one of her blogs:

I realized there was this largely untapped demographic

and decided to take the cheapest store in America, Walmart—that is stigmatized as the lowest quality in some ways—and show women struggling in the economic climate how to create something fresh and fashionable from there. The blog just kind of grew from there.

Because I wasn't just styling myself, it [her fashion design education] was kind of a grassroots apprenticeship, where I learned how to style different body types, using different kinds of clothes. That eventually helped me last year when I launched my first clothing line with Walmart because the concept was basically based on five silhouettes that flatter every woman's body type, so I had the knowledge to base that on.

One of the biggest things I've learned is understanding how important it is, as a founder, to trust your instinct. When it's really your idea that you have created, like a mother you have a sense and intuition about things. Every time I have denied it and ignored it, it's been the wrong decision. Part of the intuitive process for me is not just that it feels right; it's also based on past experience, research, analytics, and what feels true to my original idea.[12]

Like Shauna, there is something inside of you that, if unleashed, has the potential to change your world. The thing you get most excited about is worth exploring, not only for others, but for yourself.

If no one else has ever told you, I will: There is greatness inside of you and potential that is yet to be tapped. You don't

---

12 Excerpted from http://Shauna Miller, Penny Chic Founder, http://passionstori.es/fashion/

have to settle for who you are or where you are today. Life is worth so much more than just "settling." Your fulfillment in life will be to the benefit of all those connected to you, even those with whom you have no direct contact. Remember, "If you are just settling, then you lose your 'edge.'" I recently learned that from Lee Dominque, a business man speaking at a Gateway Church event. Wouldn't you say a multi-millionaire knows what he's talking about?

How do we find our life passion? It is not something that just falls into our laps. But it truly is worth putting in the work and taking time to find it out. The "work" is unfortunately the reason why so many go about their lives with no passion and are dissatisfied with the choices they make on a daily basis.

You may say, "I have no aspirations, nothing that I am that excited about." The simple answer to this common problem is *find out what makes you passionate.* Exploring brings about life experience that enables you to discover new things to love. Consider this: What could you do 24 hours a day, 7 days a week, and not get tired of it? This is key to knowing your passion.

Too many people live in a bubble. Their world is small because their vision is small. Their vision is small because their environment is small. Choose to do something different; choose to be different! It starts with a choice. Once the decision is made to find and follow your passion, you will take action.

Action always follows decision.

Passion can be birthed out of dissatisfaction in your current state, so let your discontentment be a great indication for the need for change. Previously I mentioned this quote from an executive coach, and it's worth mentioning again: "Passion and change will come when you are either excited about something or disturbed about something." Let your comfort and complacency be a silent alarm. Don't settle. If you do, it will only lead to ultimately resenting your decisions, your situation … and your life. Don't wait for your situation to change—change it! Come to the place of realization that you don't have to maintain the status quo for the rest of your life. You can do better … and you DESERVE better. Change is good; it brings about new challenges, which cause us to use skills that we may have never had to use, or never realized we had.

Growing your Passion

Passion is something both discovered and developed. Discovery is important because you must first know who you are as an individual. Remember, YOU ARE A WORTHWHILE PERSON who has value. Let those words sink in. With this revelation, you can take your first steps towards fulfillment, which can only be found when you create and give value to others.

You have value. You must believe it.

This truth must flow from your ears, to your mind, to your heart.

It is the responsibility of all people to choose what they

will believe about themselves. We need to reject the negativity of others' opinions of who we are and create a sense of worth beyond the acceptance of others. This is personal development. This is self-discovery.

I learned from our Ambitious Women's Success Coach, Amy Applebaum, that you can listen to opinions of others but you don't have to *own* them. (More about her in Chapter 15). You learn your present beliefs about yourself, then take that which is unhealthy and replace it with that which is healthy and finally develop a new healthy sense of self. Belief drives passion, and passion fuels dreams into reality. As Tony Robbins says, "Beliefs have the power to create and the power to destroy. Human beings have the awesome ability to take their life's experiences and create a meaning, one that either renders them powerless or one that can literally save their lives." While this may sound a little self-focused, it is true. The only way you can be your best for others is if you are the best you for you. It is important to be self-focused so that we learn how to relate to others in a healthy way.

One of the greatest enemies of passion is people pleasing. It will cause you to be divided within yourself. You should make every effort to resolve inner conflicts in order to be able to have focused energy toward the goals you are passionate about. There does come a time when we meet the needs of others selflessly, but it comes only after our personal needs are met. Our sense of security, both physically and emotionally, will always supersede the needs of others. It is a natural law. You are best able to help others when you are yourself satisfied and secure. Remember the airline motto:

"Secure your own oxygen mask before helping others." Do you know why they say that? It's because as the air pressure drops you have less than 30 seconds before you lose consciousness. While you wouldn't die for several minutes, you would be unconscious and unable to help anyone. That's why you need to secure your own mask first and then help those around you.

Don't be afraid of dreaming, of finding your passion. Remove from your mind everything that says, "I can't." Stop hanging around those who say, "You'll never do it." Write down what you are passionate about, the thing that fuels your dreams. While not every idea is a good one, writing your thoughts down will help you to believe that NOTHING is impossible. Every idea is doable.

With passion comes motivation. Motivation in the right direction is a passion that produces results. When you are passionate, you will be more willing to take risks. And only with great risks can you have great reward.

Take your journal out and list the things you are passionate about. Why do these things "move" you? How are you "connected" to them? What would you like to be more passionate about and why aren't you?

To stay the course of an Ambitious Woman BE PASSIONATE!

Barbara Walters is an Ambitious Woman. You can be one too.

LIVE A PASSIONATE LIFE!

Chapter 14

Live a Confident Life

Believe in Yourself And Others Will Too

Sarah Palin

Politics aside, and regardless of whether you agree with her or not, you simply MUST admire Sarah Palin's tenacity, her stick-to-it-iveness, and her confidence. Imagine getting up on stage at the Republican Convention, standing bold and strong, and delivering an amazing speech. Imagine addressing the party's convention in St. Paul, and depicting yourself as "just your average hockey mom." My absolute favorite quote from her is, "You know what the only difference between a hockey mom and a pit bull is? LIPSTICK!" I LOVE IT!

Now that's confidence!

Her confidence allowed her to become the youngest and first female governor of Alaska, the second woman to run for Vice President on a major US party ticket, and the first Republican female Vice Presidential candidate. She told

ABC's Charles Gibson that she didn't hesitate when asked to join the ticket, and she felt prepared to run the country if necessary. "I'm ready," she said. "I answered him 'yes' because I have the confidence in that readiness and knowing that you can't blink."[13]

*****

The first year in my business, I faced my first big disappointment. In fact, it devastated me. A great couple came into my business. This couple had everything it took to be successful. They were even instrumental in helping me get promoted! But the business didn't move fast enough for them. The thought never crossed my mind that they would leave, because we had become such good friends. But they decided to move on, and my confidence was shaken. But I soon learned it was just the nature of the business. (I hear the couple is now very successful in another company, and I am happy for them.) We all learned a lot together in the beginning, but we just took different paths.

Six years later, a similar situation occurred. A very special couple I had known for five years—people whose friendship I valued, whom I had helped financially, and had been a confidant to in times of emotional and spiritual crisis—decided to leave for another company. I was heartbroken. I never received a phone call from either of them, only text

13 Read more at: http://www.biography.com/people/sarah-palin-360398#media-star&awesm=~oFbBFOBpS2jooT

messages. While I realize that people have different roads to take, and they may not lead to the same place, I would have preferred to have talked it out first; but it just didn't happen.

In both situations, my confidence was shaken, but I had to rally myself. I had to "discipline my disappointments" as I've learned to say. I could not place my self-assurance or my success in other people; I simply had to find that well of confidence inside myself. One of the things that helped me was to remember why I had started my own business. As an outgoing person, I had been approached by dozens of people over the years with networking business opportunities. But none of them fit who I was. Yet I could "see" myself working in that type of industry. I knew I would be helping other people, not just making a paycheck. The fact that I was helping others to build their future is the very thing I had to refocus on when I was so down in the dumps. I had to tell myself that everyone has choices, and as long as I was doing what I could to help, I had to be satisfied with that. In both situations I've told you about, I had to take a deep breath, refocus, and remind myself that my confidence is in my own ability, not someone else's.

You Are Confident

Confidence is the feeling or belief that you can rely on someone or something. It is certainty of a truth. It is a self-assurance and appreciation of your own abilities or qualities. With it, you can accomplish great things. Without it, you are crippled with fear and halted from reaching your full potential. As the late Eleanor Roosevelt said, "We gain strength, and courage, and confidence by each experience in which we really stop to look fear in the face … we must do that which we think we cannot."

Your level of confidence is foundational to your every success. What would you do in life if you knew with all certainty that you would not fail? You would be unstoppable! Your confidence would give you all the courage you needed to succeed.

I'd like you to repeat this out loud three times: I AM UNSTOPPABLE! I would like you to write this in your journal and then write it out on a piece of paper and tape it on your bathroom mirror. Now repeat it several times each morning as you get ready for your day. It will really be weird at first, but who cares? You're the only one looking, and YOU ARE UNSTOPPABLE!

The greater your confidence, the bigger your dreams are; and the more you desire more for others and yourself, the more your entire world changes. You go for that promotion, or start that business. You invest in your future. You take more risks. There are no ideas *not* worth exploring.

With more confidence, you are more attractive to others. People have greater trust in you, and you are sought out for advice and leadership; your thinking changes in terms of solutions instead of problems.

Confidence breeds happiness and contentment. It gives you a sense of control in your life, which leads to greater levels of emotional security. In fact, HAVING CONFIDENCE

WILL SET YOU APART FROM EVERYONE ELSE.

You Can Do It

I have had countless people tell me, "I wish I had the confidence you do." Well, they can—and you can too! The good news is that this kind of confidence can be built and developed. You start with changing your mindset. Yes, you can do this! Choose today to silence the voices that say, "You can't." Every time you are tempted to say, "I can't," instead say, "I can!" You can choose to see that every experience in your life has purpose and can help you succeed in every endeavor. Yes, I am talking to you! You should be realistic in your views of what you know and what you can stand to learn. Just know that there is always room for growth. And as long as you are willing to put in the work, you should have confidence that you can accomplish anything.

Look upon every step you take as a learning experience. Every mistake and every failure can be viewed as a stepping stone to success. Confidence will cause you to face your fears of failure. Have courage to make mistakes and pull yourself up. Pull up your spanx, learn your lessons, and keep trying.

Confidence is the result of your mindset as it relates to your actions.

So say it one more time: I AM UNSTOPPABLE!

I encourage you to face every fear in order to develop confidence. It will take time and persistence to learn that you have within you the power to overcome anything, if you believe you can. Practice will calm your nervousness. If you believe in yourself, you will continue to practice until perfect. Don't fall short of this important key because of laziness or fatigue. Too many people use that as an excuse to stop trying. Don't become one of them.

Here is something that is so true, something I want you, as a woman, to know about yourself. It is written by someone who must be an Ambitious Woman, Tia Sparkles Singh:

You.Are.Amazing.

As. You. Are.

Stronger than you know.

More beautiful than you think.

Worthier than you believe.

More loved than you can ever imagine. Passionate about making a difference. Fiery when protecting those you love.

Learning. Growing. Not alone.

Warm. Giving. Generous. Quirky. Sexy. Funny. Smart. Flawed. Whole. Scared. Brave. And so, so, so. much. more.[14]

14 Be Strong. Be Confident. Be You. ~ Copyright: Tia Sparkles Singh, 2011. http://www.yourlifeyourway.net/2011/10/10/75-most-empowering- inspirational-quotes-for-sassy-kickass-women/

Now that's something to write in your journal. Then write it on a piece of paper and put it somewhere so you can see and read it EVERY day!

As an Ambitious Woman, you are a woman of action! With action comes momentum. Once the ball is rolling, there is nothing that can stop you. You are your best asset, your best friend, and your biggest supporter. Remember, action will always silence negativity.

In a moment of uncertainty, get your body in motion and change your state of mind. Physical activity—whether at the gym, at home, or at your place of business—is the best way to shut your brain off from negativity. Go for a run or walk. Choose not to be defeated by old or negative mindsets. Choose to take action against all distractions and lack of motivation. When you are in tough situations, remember Diana Nyad's mantra, "Find a way." Don't let anyone or anybody stop you from finding a way to accomplish what you want to do.

Overcome Your Self-Talk

Another key to building confidence is to recognize and understand your self-defeating self-talk. Self-talk is the endless chatter, the continuous monologue, that runs through your mind. Your self-talk controls your feelings, and your feelings control your actions and reactions. Negative self-talk is crippling; it leads to all kinds of negative emotions, which paralyze you so that you cannot do anything. It's important to "war" against this type of self-talk with positive affirmations and to focus on the good and positive.

Here is a truth: *Something is only as scary as your mind tells you it is.* Tell yourself that you can handle it—because you can! There are enough people in the world that will tell us we can't. Don't join the crowd of negativity against yourself. Tell yourself that you can. Develop healthy and positive self-talk on a regular basis, and your level of confidence will begin to soar.

What you believe you will say. What you say you will do.

What you do will become a habit.

Giving to Others

By now you know that I've always been an encourager. I love pouring myself into others and seeing them accomplish their goals. Helping others is a great way to build confidence. It has been said that the best way to learn something is to teach it. When you build others up, you can use the same principles to build yourself up. The good results in others will be attributed to you, which will build your confidence.

Accept Yourself

I encourage you to accept yourself as you are. Be realistic about who you are. The things that you feel need to change, change them. But celebrate the things that are good as well.

As we grow, the view that we have of ourselves is developed by our environment and the choices we make. Here is something you cannot change: You have made yourself who you are, and only you can change who you are. Take control of what you think and believe about yourself. Choose to love who you are and stay on a path of personal development. Trust in yourself that you can do anything. Confidence says that nothing is impossible for the person who believes.

If you think you can or you think you can't, either way you are correct.

As an Ambitious Woman, YOU ARE CONFIDENT!

Sarah Palin is an Ambitious Woman. You can be one too.

LIVE A CONFIDENT LIFE!

Chapter 15

Live an Accountable Life

Everyone Needs to Be Accountable

I have worked hard enough and have been blessed enough to be recognized amongst my peers in a large billion-dollar company. I have also been fortunate enough to have achieved the highest position, as well as be a top money earner for ten years in a row. I speak in cities locally and throughout the country where my company has a presence. And almost everywhere I go, people come up to me and ask, "How did you do it? What words of wisdom do you have for me?"

I'm sure that many of them think I have some magical formula that guarantees success. And I really wish I had a magic wand to help them. But I have to tell the truth: "Be accountable to someone. Have a mentor or get a coach, but be accountable."

Most often people look as if to say, "That's it?"

I find myself wanting to tell them John Maxwell's words, "People want to do what I do, but they don't want to do what I do." Did you get that? That's because successful people do what unsuccessful people will NOT do.

As an Ambitious Woman, I believe the most important

thing you can do to begin your journey towards success is to "be accountable." What does it mean to be accountable? How do you become accountable?

I classify being accountable into three sections: 1) having an accountability partner; 2) finding a mentor; 3) hiring a coach. All three are necessary to have the maximum success.

Have an accountability partner. This is the first place to start, and it is the most crucial to your success. This person is not your coach. She is *holding you accountable* to the things you said you were going to do and not letting you off the hook when you don't.

Finding an accountability partner is probably one of the easiest things you'll do in your business, and for your life, so why not do it first thing? There is something about us as people that says, "I don't want to let someone else down." We might let ourselves off the hook, but we don't want to embarrass ourselves in front of someone else by not following through on what we've said we would do. Set your goals, and then find someone to help you be accountable to keeping them. After all, *you* said you wanted to achieve these goals, so they aren't setting them for you nor are they going to tell you what to do.

When looking for an accountability partner, the question always comes up, "Who is the best partner?" Here are a few tips I found:

- *Conversational but confidential.* You want someone who is willing to listen to you and talk about the details of your goals. But you don't want someone who will break confidentiality and share your "business" with others.

- *Challenging but not condemning.* The person you choose should not be hard and critical, waiting for you to make mistakes and then pointing them out. Choose someone who is willing to challenge and advise you, and even confront you when necessary, but above all someone who encourages you.
- Ask your potential partners if they are *willing to hold you accountable.* If not, there is no sense having them in this role. Ask them if they *want* to accept the responsibility. Be prepared for some to say no, and then find someone else.
- *Who should it be?* A spouse may be too close to give you constructive feedback—or may want to give you too much! But if you ask your spouse, let him decide. And don't take it personally if he says "No"! My husband does not want to be my partner, as I would probably take everything too personally. That's okay. Even if your spouse decides he wants to, it is usually best to have at least one accountability partner of the same gender.

I hold an Ambitious Women's Conference every year, and one part that everyone enjoys the most is when the women find a buddy or a "sister" with whom they can communicate with the following year. We do the same in the "Ambitious Women's Success and Mentoring Club." All of the women are encouraged to have an accountability partner while in the program, and we have our own private Facebook page where the women can get support from their "buddies." This is also one of the best things about the club.

I encourage you: If you *do not* have an accountability partner, please get one now! Don't wait. It doesn't cost anything and you have everything to gain.

Find a Mentor. About mentoring, Oprah Winfrey said, "A mentor is someone who allows you to see the hope inside yourself." That's powerful! When I look back on my life, I wish I would have had more mentors. In one respect, I had mentors—my parents, a few relatives, Sunday School teachers, and other adults who taught me life skills. But I never sought out people while growing up because I was too independent, too set on doing "life" my way. Now that isn't a bad thing; I love living life on my terms. But I can also see why having personal mentors would have been extremely helpful.

Believe it or not, you have mentors in your life that you might not know, or may not have a strong personal relationship with. All of us should have several. These are people we "admire from a distance" like an author who writes inspirational books that you relate to, or a pastor, co- worker, or political figure. For example, I consider John Maxwell one of my mentors. I read all his books, and I get something out of every one of them and try to apply these lessons to my life. Although I have had the privilege of meeting him on several occasions, I don't have a personal relationship with him.

I also consider my pastor, Robert Morris of Gateway Church, to be a mentor because I listen to all of his sermons and read all of his books. He has a lot of influence in my personal and spiritual life on a weekly basis. Although he might know who I am, we do not have a personal relationship. Mentors like these can change for you as you go through the different seasons and circumstances of your life. You can choose to follow them and gain from them at any time.

However, it wasn't until I started into the business world on straight commission sales that I met my first personal mentor. I've already told you about Bill and the positive effects he has had on developing my business skills. I've also told you about Lesley, who has been a great friend and mentor. But having a personal mentor earlier on who would have taught me about life, about how to deal effectively with other people, and how to develop what I call "win-win" relationships—that would have been such a great help to me, and perhaps I would have achieved success a lot quicker.

What Is Mentoring?

Mentoring is not a deep, scary term. A mentor is someone who helps guide your life. They offer you their life experience, knowledge, skills, and perspective, either in general terms about life or specifically in business, finances, faith, or other topics.

But mentoring is more than just about what someone can do for you; it's about relationship. The more time you spend with your mentor, the deeper your relationship will develop. A mentor will help you believe in yourself and boost your confidence in your skills and abilities. A mentor will help you grow in confidence and provide guidance and support. Having a mentor will make you more self-aware so that you can take responsibility for your direction in life, so that you can plan with purpose. We all have a need for insight that is outside of our normal life and educational experience. Mentoring creates a one-of-a-kind opportunity for collaboration, goal achievement, and problem solving.

Mentoring itself can be looked at as the transfer of wisdom from a trusted counselor, normally in a leadership position, who helps to direct your career path. A good mentor will care deeply for you and will go out of her way to help you succeed and fulfill your potential.

Types of Mentoring

There are two types of mentoring. The first is *informal.* This is what most people think of when they think of mentoring: a spontaneous, casual relationship where a senior person takes a junior person "under his or her wing" and provides long-term guidance and counsel.

The second is *structured.* These are programs designed to create a culture where people can proactively support the development of others and each other. In these programs, mentors are generally matched to support specific goals such as leadership development or retention. Generally mentoring involves meeting with a junior person on a one- on-

one basis. They have to be someone you absolutely respect, admire, and are willing to listen to their counsel.

Everyone needs help along the way in our careers and their personal lives, so it just makes sense to have mentors, people older and wiser, in our lives. They are models we can look up to.

Things to Look For

- *Willingness to Share*

Look for a mentor who is willing to teach what she knows and someone who will accept you where you are in life. Look for someone who remembers what it was "like to be in your shoes."

- *A Positive Mindset*

Your mentor should be a positive role model and someone who is upbeat.

- *Personal Interest*

Good mentors have strong communication skills. They want to empower you to be the best you can be.

- *Guidance and Feedback*

Your mentor should be a good sounding board for you. Her role isn't to tell you what to do but to provide guidance and feedback so you can make your own decisions.

- *Respect*

Not only should your mentor respect you as a person, but she should also be respected in her area of expertise.

- *Goal Setting*

It is not always easy to figure out what you want to do, so your mentor should help you do this and help you set goals to achieve what you have set out to do.

- *Objective*

Mentors offer their views and opinions. But they also are willing to listen to what you have to say. In fact, listening is probably the most important skill a good mentor will have.

- *Good Question*

Asking good questions will help you figure out where you are right now and where you wantto be. They help you clarify your goals and what you want to achieve.

Hire a Success or Personal Coach Oh no!Now we are going to talk about spending money. And that means commitment, sacrifice. Delayed gratification! Sometimes a coach and mentor is the same person, but they are people you hire to help you. Depending on your financial resources, you can hire one at different levels. It might not be in your budget when you first start out, which is why you can find a "free" mentor you respect and admire. But as soon as you can, hire a mentor/coach, no matter what. I promise you, it will be the best investment you ever make in your business and yourself. From the beginning, make this part of your business overhead expense. *Invest money in yourself.* You are worth it. If I had the choice of spending money on advertising my service or hiring a coach, I would pick a coach hands down; most likely, they will help and guide me to find and earn the money needed for the advertising budget. That's what they do; they pay for themselves in the long run.

It has just been in the last couple of years I have seen the value of hiring a mentor/coach. But I wish I would have had the foresight to do this much earlier. I really didn't know much about what these people do. Then I met a personal business coach, whom I thought would be perfect for my son, Peter, who had just finished college. He needed someone to guide him in his decisions, to help him get a plan and set goals, and to prepare for the world. (Sometimes parents really are NOT the best ones to do that, as our children may hear it better from someone else.) So I hired her to coach him. I just thought it was a good idea for my son, but not for me. I didn't need one! I knew what I was doing.

Then she sent me a video featuring Eric Schmidt, the CEO of Google. When asked about the best advice he was ever given, he replied, "Have a coach." At first, Mr. Schmidt had the same reaction I did. Told by a board member he needed a coach, he replied, "I don't need a coach. I'm an established CEO; is something wrong? Why do I need a coach?" The board member said, "EVERYONE needs a coach." Then Eric went on to say that one thing people are never good at is seeing themselves as others see them. Every famous athlete and every famous performer has a coach; I started to think about that.

Aaron, my oldest son, has played baseball since he was five years old, all the way through college. And every season, he had a coach—someone who trained him, who showed him how to play, and taught what to do and what not to do. They saw things in him that he could not see in himself. Even as a young player, he was being coached, and every year he got better and better. We spent money sending him to baseball school, camps, and select teams. That is perhaps one of the reasons he was such a great ball player and could play in college; he had a lot of coaching.

But I never put it together that having coaching in business would work the same way. Think about all the money you may have spent paying for a coach for your children in sports, dance, singing, music, you name it. And the longer they had a coach, the better they became at their chosen activity.

If you follow the business world, you will also hear Bill Gates say over and over, "Everyone needs a coach." I had heard that, but I honestly thought that was only for rich and famous people. However, the more I looked into coaching, I saw it was for everyone, and the more I saw I needed it.

I mentioned before that sometimes if you aren't proactive in your pursuit, God will allow things into your life to get your attention. Well, soon after I hired a coach for my son, I was introduced to a high-level coach and mentor, Eli Davidson. She has even been a coach for Joan Rivers and appeared on a reality show with her. So I hired her to help me for a short time to get some direction. In just a few phone conversations and a long day in California, I realized the vision for my legacy and what I was created to do. She gave me the encouragement and support to write this book. She started by telling me to write for 15 minutes a day, every day, and soon I would have a book. Now how profound is that! Was it worth all the money I paid her? You bet! That was a priceless experience.

Shortly after, I was introduced to Amy Applebaum, a leading success coach. Amy has helped thousands of female entrepreneurs around the world break through barriers that were inhibiting their success and happiness through her "Release Your Inner Millionairess" coaching club. As a CEO, business coach, wife, mom and 18-year entrepreneur, she understands the challenges of running your own business as well as the fears and doubts that come along. Amy's success has landed her on almost every major media outlet, including ABC news, CNN, TLC, Dr. Drew's Lifechangers and Martha Stewart Radio. She has also contributed to *New York Times*, *Cosmopolitan*, *Figure*, *Shape,* and *Woman's World.*

Wow!

But even without all of Amy's accolades, when we first met, our spirits and our hearts connected immediately. She had a passion for helping women entrepreneurs, and so did I. She had all the expertise and experience, and I had a following of women. Together, we formed the "Ambitious Women Success and Mentoring Club," which has been one of the most amazing experiences for me and for all the women that have joined. In just a few short months, we had hundreds of women joining and dozens of testimonials of victories and promotions and success from Amy's mentoring.

If you have mentors and coaches in your life, you are in very unique company. While many people talk about the need for mentoring, few people actually seek out a mentor or hire a coach, and fewer still want to mentor other people. So that presents a big problem.

Once you have a mentor and you realize all the benefits of having one, I challenge you to be a mentor for someone else. That will help you to grow even more. They say the teacher always learns the most. Well, mentors have almost as much to gain as the one they are mentoring. And it really does help you stay on course with your own life.

But before I close, I want to tell you a little bit more about Amy Applebaum, whom we call "the Baum," and how she discovered mentoring and coaching!

*****

In 1998, I launched my very first business, which involved vending machines. I had NO IDEA what I was doing. I didn't know what a business plan was. I didn't know how to raise money. I didn't know anything about sales, branding, marketing, administration, taxes … you name it, I didn't know it!

The first six months were a nightmare. Zero accounts, as in NO VENDING MACHINES PLACED IN ANY LOCATIONS. I had no idea what I was doing wrong. I was broke. Then I placed my first vending machine in the local donut shop— filled with kids! YES! I was so excited. I ran out and bought a bottle of five-dollar champagne to celebrate. Just as I was about to pop the cork off the bottle, the manager from the donut shop called. My sticker machine had fallen on a little boy. He was hanging on the coin mechanism and pulled the 120 lb. unit right down on top of him!

"Fear and negative thoughts rushed through my mind in an instant:

- Is the boy okay?
- Oh my god … what happens if he isn't?
- How will I pay for his medical bills?
- I knew I didn't mount that stand properly—why didn't I ask for help?
- Why didn't I get business insurance?
- OMG! I can't believe I lost my first account.
- I am such an idiot.
- I almost killed a little boy.
- My business is OVER!
- I am freaking out!

This was one of the scariest moments of my life. And this was the day that I put my pride and 'I can do it myself' attitude aside, once and for all.

That's when the whole 'universe of success' opened up for me. I found someone to help me, to mentor me, and to show me the way.

I went from one vending machine to 300 in one year. YES! And, I made a ton of mistakes but, I was *doing* it and I had support. Phew! Why did I think I could do it alone? You know, the basic stuff. I didn't want to bother anyone. I believed I could handle it. Yada. Yada. Yada.

Today I am building my 100-million-dollar dream company. I have a bad-ass team! And there is NO WAY that I could do this without them, nor would I want to! Team makes it real. Team makes it fun. Team makes it possible!

If I had one piece of advice for all the Ambitious Women out there, it would be this: Put together a team of mentors, right now! And as you grow, get new mentors that can help you achieve your goals. You are as successful as the people you put yourself around … end of discussion!"

*****

You gotta just love Amy. She just tells it like it is. So, who are your mentors? Who do you admire, respect? Write their names in your journal. Then it will get exciting as you start to look for personal mentors and coaches to help you get where you want to go. If you are not accountable to someone, what is holding you back? What is your greatest fear in being accountable? What do you see as the greatest benefit? How do you hold yourself accountable?

Remember, to be an Ambitious Woman, BE ACCOUNTABLE!

Amy Applebaum is an Ambitious Woman. You can be one too.

LIVE AN ACCOUNTABLE LIFE!

Chapter 16

Live Your Choices

Be Responsible For Your Own Life

Well, you know by now that I love shoes! The more varieties, the better! In every city I go to, whether I'm speaking at an event, networking my business, or just vacationing, I seek out the big shoe stores and the little boutiques. I love having so many choices!

Choices are a part of life (even when they don't involve shoes). From the moment we wake up to the time we go to bed, we are continually making choices. Do we get up at a certain time or sleep in? What should we eat? What road to work should we take? What's for lunch? Dinner? Should I watch a TV show or read a book? Most of our daily choices are simple to make (except when going shoe shopping!).

I learned a great deal about choices and how they can compound in your life from Darren Hardy, former publisher of *Success* Magazine. In my copy of his book *The Compound Effect*, I highlighted what he said about choices such as, "Everything in your life exists because you first made a choice about something. Choices are at the root of every one of your results. Each choice starts a behavior that over time becomes a habit." Now that's worth thinking about and writing in your journal.

But what about choices that really change our lives … how do we make these types of choices when we have little or no idea how they will affect us?

I'm sure you know the story of *Alice in Wonderland.*

Alice faced a similar dilemma:

Alice came to a fork in the road. "Which road do I take?" she asked.

"Where do you want to go?" responded the Cheshire Cat.

"I don't know," Alice answered. "Then," said the Cat, "it doesn't matter."

Alice in Wonderland, by Lewis Carroll

We have all been in Alice's shoes (hmmm, those are shoes I don't want!). She had a choice but didn't know what she wanted. She had no direction, no vision, so she could not determine what road to take, which way to go. When it comes to choices that will affect our lives, we cannot rush into a decision … but we cannot deliberate for too long either, or else, we will find ourselves left standing at the fork in the road with life passing us by. However, the importance of making good choices cannot be overstated.

Let's look at another story we all know, *The Wizard of Oz*. Dorothy had a choice to return home to Kansas, simply by clicking her heels three times. The choice to do so allowed her to go home. At the beginning of the movie, she had another choice to make. She could remain a captive of the Wicked Witch of the West or she could follow the Good Witch of the South, who told Dorothy that her slippers were so powerful, anything she wished for was possible, even without the help of the Wizard. (Hmm, those are the shoes I want!)

As Ambitious Women, we understand—or we should understand—that WE ARE RESPONSIBLE FOR OUR CHOICES. Statements like "He made me" or "She forced me" cannot be part of our vocabulary. Even the Wicked Witch of the West could not force Dorothy to do anything. While we may not have a choice in everything (If your boss gives you an assignment to do, you cannot tell him/her, "Sorry, I'm doing my nails right now."), when it comes to who we are, who we want to become, and what we want to do in life, we have the POWER TO CHOOSE! Just like the Good Witch of the South told Dorothy that *anything* she wished for was possible!

Consider these great quotes from women who have achieved much in life and write them in your journal:

> "It is our choices … that show what we truly are,
> far more than our abilities."
>
> **– J. K. Rowling**

"One's philosophy is not best expressed in words; it is expressed in the choices one makes … and the choices we make are ultimately our responsibility."

– Eleanor Roosevelt

"I believe that we are solely responsible for our choices, and we have to accept the consequences of every deed, word, and thought throughout our lifetime."

– Elisabeth Kübler-Ross

"I think happiness is a choice. If you feel yourself being happy and can settle in to the life choices you make, then it's great. It's really, really great. I swear to God, happiness is the best makeup."

– Drew Barrymore

"I think that God gives you your own will and choices. I don't believe that we're supposed to drag ourselves through life defeated and not see God's blessings. But you have to make the right choices and follow that still, small voice within you. Because I think that's how God leads us."

– Joel Osteen

Choices, Choices

I was watching TV one evening, and a commercial for Dove chocolate came on. It was very inviting. The chocolate looked delicious. The woman eating it was gorgeous, and oh my, was she enjoying that piece of dark chocolate! Immediately I thought, *I've got to have some chocolate!* Then I sighed. I knew that one piece would lead to another, would lead to another, would lead … you get where I'm going. My point is this: as much as I love chocolate, it doesn't like me! It goes straight to my hips, my waist, my everywhere! So I had to NOT make a choice that would have a detrimental effect on me.

Part of the problem with choosing poorly is the tendency to choose immediate gratification rather than delayed reward. Another problem is ignoring risks because of the lure of large reward. One pitfall is an impulse problem; the other is a lack of reality and understanding consequences. For example, had I chosen to eat just one piece of Dove chocolate, I would have given myself immediate gratification. But I know myself, and the other pieces I would have eaten would have got me in trouble. Here is a truth: Ambitious Women know themselves and are willing, in most cases (except when choosing shoes!), to reap the benefits of delayed rewards over the fleeting feeling that immediate gratification brings. Does that make sense?

Choices and Values

What you value will be a great contributor to the choices you make. Are you a family woman? Do you love solitude?

Do you value others' opinions or prefer to "go it alone"? The word *value* can be defined as "an emotional state or character attribute that you desire to live within or be defined by." For instance, I value the feeling of being in control; it makes me feel secure and confident; I love the value of being alone at times, it gives me a great sense of calm and peace. I also love the feeling of being independent; I feel free and empowered.

As Ambitious Women, when we understand our values, we have a better understanding of what is driving us towards certain behaviors, and why we make particular choices. The big choices in life, the big-picture ones, will be dictated by what you believe in. If you have faith in God, your religious values will determine much of what you do in life. If you have faith in humanity, your belief that all people are basically good will shape your choices.

Your values will impact your choices, no matter what you base your values on. If you don't have something to believe in, like Alice, you won't know which way to choose—and it won't matter.

Choosing to Act

I had a choice way back when in 2006 to change my financial destiny. My son, David, walked into my office and asked me to take "a look" at a business opportunity. My first response was NO! That was pretty ignorant. The truth is that people don't always know what they don't know, and that includes me. So, we should always be willing to keep our options open before we make a choice to say NO.

Fortunately for me, David was persistent and, after several trips to my office, I finally made the choice to "look." That day forever changed the financial destiny of my and my family's future. Fast forward, and I can tell you that going into that business opportunity was the best decision I have ever made! But after I made the choice to look, I had to make the choice to ACT.

The big choices are like freeways—they'll get you in the direction you want to go, really fast. We all have to make them. But if you choose to not act, you will never accomplish your goals and you may become guilty of procrastinating. If you refuse to act, you may lose out on something you have always wanted or needed to do.

You can choose deliberately. Remember this statement. YOU CAN CHOOSE DELIBERATELY.

From now on, this is how you'll make choices. You'll be deliberate. You'll look at the choice with your preferred end result in mind. You'll weigh risks and rewards. You'll rule out choices until you've arrived at the one you feel is right.

Changing Your Choices

So what happens when you make a wrong choice? You could forge straight ahead and let your life "right" itself or even "keel over," or you might go back to where you started and make a different choice. Or, you could abandon the choice and make a new one, rather than try to work through the problems that arise after your first unwise choice.

I have always believed in making a choice one time and living with the consequences—I believe in decisiveness. But I also know that sometimes your best efforts don't prevail, and you have to let go. Making a wrong choice is not the end of the world, but you need to analyze what went wrong. Then you can consider your options moving forward, consult someone with experience, dust yourself off, and make another choice.

Seek the input of people WHO know, not people YOU know, just like Dorothy did with the Good Witch. Always consider the end result when you're making choices. Choose deliberately. Be patient, not impulsive. Keep the big picture in mind, and don't be afraid to change your choices.

From one Ambitious Woman to another, I challenge you to write in your journal all of the ambitious choices you have in front of you, based on who you are, on your terms, and according to your values. As you consider each one, write down what you need to do to accomplish each choice. Remember, YOU HAVE CHOICES!

You can be an Ambitious Woman.

CHOOSE YOUR LIFE AND LIVE YOUR CHOICE!

Chapter 17

It's All in Your Attitude

You CAN Do It!

We are all familiar with Mother Teresa and her great work with the poor during her lifetime. But consider some of the things she went through:

- Her father died when she was eight.
- At age 18 she left home and never saw her family again.
- She lived among the poorest of the poor in India.
- She was plagued her entire life with doubt and loneliness, including grave misgivings about her entire mission in life.[15]

What kept Mother Teresa going in the face of some of life's harshest trials? While I never knew her, it is obvious to me that she had great faith in God, and she CHOSE to maintain a positive attitude. Despite everything, she chose to be cheerful, hopeful, and compassionate. These traits became the hallmark attitudes of her life.

---

15 For more information see: http://www.biography.com/people/mother- teresa-9504160#awesm=~oFeVXkZGk0kbEy

You need attitudes. I need attitudes. We all need attitudes! And I mean that. What I don't mean is attitudes of arrogance, entitlement, or of "I'm all that." What we need are attitudes of assurance, of capability, "can do" attitudes.

Having a good, positive, and healthy attitude is so different from being arrogant. However others see us is determined by their own perspective, so we may indeed appear "better than others." So, we do need to be careful of the words we speak, the tone we use, and the intent behind our speech. Because I am outgoing and confident, I know sometimes people misinterpret my intentions and are intimidated by me. I am still working on that part, because I do not want people to get the idea that I think I am better than them. I know I am not.

Developing an Attitude

Our attitude comes from our thought processes; they can be positive or negative depending upon our outlook. Thus, you can say that your perception greatly influences your attitude, views, and opinions.

Obviously, our attitudes are big parts of our behavior and decision making. However, we LEARN our attitudes; they aren't just inborn. How often have you heard, or said, "She acts just like her mother." Have you ever wondered how someone learns to act like her parent? We learn by observing and experiencing our parents' actions, attitudes, and behaviors. It was a rude awakening when I saw my young children act out some of my bad behaviors. Now that they are adults,

I am apologetic about some of the wrong behaviors that I passed on to them. But you know, that is the past, and we can never live in the past. Because of my openness, and their awareness to good and bad attitudes, both of my sons are terrific parents and great role models. My point is that we are impacted by those in authority in our lives. We can learn to be capable and confident, or flighty and irresponsible.

Attitude in the Making

Think about your life and times when you were just plain down and your world was a dark place. I already told you that I've been there: losing a child, losing a business, trading in property for a vehicle, having to take food packages. However, my never-give-up attitude has pulled me through these trials and more.

When we get down, we can't seem to find our way out. We get stuck in a downward spiral that seems all- consuming until we find relief, or until WE change.

The first thing we can do to help ourselves is to change our attitude.

Now think about a time when you were feeling good and how your attitude affected your life. Here is a truth: Even when situations are painful, you can choose a positive attitude. You know that saying, "When life hands you lemons, make lemonade"? That's a positive attitude. It's not denying and avoiding the negative; it's learning how to handle yourself, and the situation, from a different viewpoint.

Is this easy? Not necessarily. However, we can change our mindsets and our attitudes and that's the message I want you to hear.

We can MAKE THE DECISION TO CHANGE OUR ATTITUDE!

Time to Change

I realize it is hard to change. We are comfortable with ourselves, including the negative side of us. So what is involved in that change?

You are!

It's not some magical thing that has to happen—it all begins with you. You have the power to change your attitude and your perceptions, any time you choose. As you do, you will discover that these changes bring you increased happiness and joy and that you feel empowered and capable.

You might be asking, "How do I go about making these changes and changing my attitude?" The answer is— with awareness, and with insight, and with watching others you consider role models. They could be people at church, at work, a friend, neighbor, or family member. Find people who exhibit a positive attitude, and watch them closely. How do they do it? How do they keep a cheerful face in, even during, tough times? How do they make lemonade out of life's lemons?

I have a cousin, Carmela. Well, she is not my real cousin, except by marriage, but she might as well be. Our husbands are cousins, and they are so much alike; it is easy to see the Italian side in both of them. But then Carmela and I are so much alike, and we didn't even come from the same family; we both developed attitudes. She has one of the best attitudes of anyone I know. Oh, she can get upset and want things changed or corrected, but she does it all with the right attitude. Her aggressive attitudes always come full circle to positive and encouraging ones. She makes great lemonade with her lemons. But, what else would I expect? She is on my Italian-New York side of the family.

We can also learn the importance of how attitude affects our life through people like Joni Eareckson Tada, the Founder and CEO of Joni and Friends International Disability Center, an international advocate for people with disabilities. A diving accident in 1967 left Joni Eareckson, then 17, a quadriplegic in a wheelchair. During her rehabilitation, Joni learned how to paint with a brush between her teeth. Her high-detail fine art paintings and prints are now world-famous.[16]

Have you heard of Nick Vujicic? He was born with no legs or arms and just a little "flipper" on one foot. He refused to allow these disabilities to dictate his life. Today he travels around the world, encouraging people from all backgrounds. His blog title describes his commitment to never giving up: *Attitude is Altitude!* In it he writes, "Dream big, my friend, and never give up. We all make mistakes, but none of us are mistakes. Take one day at a time. Embrace the positive attitudes,

---

16 For more information see: http://www.joniandfriends.org/jonis- corner/jonis-bio/

perspectives, principles, and truths I share, and you too will overcome."[17]

So, how do you get this kind of attitude? Here are some things you can do to cultivate a change of attitude.

- Admit it

When you are feeling down or having a bad day and your attitude stinks, then admit it to yourself. Don't live in denial. Admitting something takes away the "control" it has in your life. Once you've accepted there is an issue, you can decide to make a change.

- Get some rest

How many mornings have you woken up and thought, "Ugh, I need to get more sleep." You are overworked and overstressed, and the day hasn't even started! How do you feel? I'll bet you are in a lousy mood, and the smallest things can set you off. You know how I know that? Because that's me when I don't get enough sleep. Taking the time to rest and forcing ourselves to take a break can often be the best thing we can do. Rest and sleep are vital to maintaining a positive attitude.

- Get clarity

You are in a bad mood, but you are not sure why. Is it because of something at work? Someone at home? Something you have done? You may not be feeling quite right, but try to figure out what is bothering you. Until you do, you will

---

17 Read more at: http://www.attitudeisaltitude.com/about-nick-his-story

have a bad attitude. Take some time to reflect and ponder. Whatever is bothering you will soon surface, and you can change your attitude when you decide what to do.

- Consider the consequences

Are you stressed out because of a deadline? Are you taking your attitude out on your kids or your spouse? Consider the consequences. The deadline will pass, but you will continue to live with your family. Why should they take the brunt of your ugliness? How will they act towards you? They may not understand the stress you are under, but they sure understand your ugly attitude. And if things get worse at home, your attitude will get worse as well. So get clear on the consequences of your bad attitude, and decide to change! Just so you know, this is one area I have to work on constantly. It seems I am always on a deadline and have 20 things to do at once. I am a multi-tasker, but when I get stressed and overwhelmed I am not a fun person. Just ask anyone who lives or works with me. But my mentor, Bill, taught me a long time ago when you feel that way, just stop. Do ONLY one thing at a time. When it is finished, go on to the next. It does work, but you have to make the choice to do it that way!

- Do something to change

You are coming home after having an argument with a friend, co-worker, or boss. You know you'll have a bad attitude when you get home. So what can you do before you get there? Take a longer route home to let off some steam? Stop at a Starbucks and think things through? Call someone you trust and get "it" out? How about going for a walk or some other form of exercise? Doing something positive will quickly change the way you deal with those you love. Recently I was traveling with one of my closest friends. It was really late, and we were both tired. Things weren't going exactly as planned, and we just started snapping at each other. Finally, I left and she went to bed. That time away was what we needed to regroup, to change the situation. I felt really bad, so I went in the hotel room and woke her up not knowing if she was going to snap at me or accept me. But, I took a chance and said, "I'm sorry." She immediately said I'm sorry too, we hugged, and everything was fine!

- Change your view

We all have situations that "trigger" us. But remember, whatever ticks you off will soon be gone, and you won't remember it a year from now. It is not the situation or the person we are facing that makes us upset; it is our mindset. So we can choose to change the way we perceive and respond to someone or something. For example, if you feel like you have too much to do at home, rather than complaining and wishing it would go away, look at it as a challenge. Imagine how good you will feel after the work is finished. A positive attitude will give you confidence, courage, and an I-can-do-this attitude.

- Be thankful

Here is another favorite verse of mine from the Bible: "whatever is true, whatever is noble, whatever is right, whatever is pure, whatever is lovely, whatever is admirable—if anything is excellent or praiseworthy—think about such things." Whenever I'm in a stressful or frustrating situation, or with someone who irks me, I think about these words. Being thankful is one of the greatest and quickest ways to change your attitude. When you are thankful and express it to others, you will be amazed at how different you feel.

Living your life to the fullest is the reason you are here, and your attitude will go a long way to determine this. I encourage you to carefully consider your attitude every day. When you stay upbeat, when you see the positive, others will say, "You sure have a good attitude." Now, grab your world and make lemonade! Now, write in your journal the new attitudes you want to have. Go ahead, give yourself permission to HAVE ATTITUDES!

You have attitudes, some good and poor ones. Take out your journal and write down the attitudes you have that line up with being an Ambitious Woman. Then write out the ones that hold you back. Next, write out the good and bad attitudes that others have commented on. How can you change the negative ones?

Mother Teresa was an Ambitious Woman. You can be one too.

IT'S ALL IN YOUR ATTITUDE!

Chapter 18

Ambitious Women NEVER Arrive

It's The Journey That Matters

Congratulations! You have now become a MUCH MORE AMBITIOUS WOMAN!

Now it's time to chill a little. You might be thinking, "I have to do all of that to become the Ambitious Woman I want to be?" I hear you, sista. Becoming an Ambitious Woman *does not* happen overnight. Becoming one is a process. Repeat after me: "Becoming an Ambitious Woman is a process." It's a daily thought, a daily effort and then ... ambition will come, followed by success.

It is impossible to absorb all of this information and incorporate it into your life in a short time. Truthfully, it has taken me thirty years to make each of these traits part of my life! So take a deep breath and relax. Yes, your goal is to develop each of these traits in your life; but you have to go at your own pace.

Think about the characteristics you have read about that help define Ambitious Women everywhere, characteristics that add quality and depth to our lives. Hopefully you now understand more clearly what your abilities and talents are and know how to enhance them—and yourself—even more. You're ready to grab onto your world.

You're ready to make a difference.

Together we've learned that we are powerful and capable, that we have many skills and talents. We want to march forth, bringing others along with us, and make an impact on our world. Are we ready? Of course we are—and the next few pages summarize all we've learned and offer additional insights as we move forward.

We recognize that we want to stretch ourselves, and we have gained determination about the steps we need to follow to do this. We've learned about our ability to take action, to not just sit and wait for someone to notice our skills and push us toward them. We know how to recognize our strengths and how to utilize them as we follow our goals and dreams. We've learned from the stories of others; we've learned about courage and humility; we've learned about joy and determination. We've learned to look at ourselves differently than before and how to value who we are.

Is there a next step? Of course.

We want to continue to grow, to tap into our potential, and to realize how strong we are. As Marissa Mayer, CEO of Yahoo, said, "I always did something I was a little not ready to do. I think that's how you grow. When there's that moment of 'Wow, I'm not really sure I can do this,' and you push through those moments, that's when you have a breakthrough."

I'm sure you can relate to that! We don't always feel ready and prepared, we're not always positive that we know how to proceed. What we can do is to ACT as if we are confident in ourselves because, ultimately, we are. We PUSH THROUGH into success. There is no going back, no retreat, just because of a minute of self-doubt. We refuse to allow ourselves to be frozen and paralyzed by thoughts. We give ourselves permission to grab on and accomplish the task.

As Ambitious Women, I am here to remind you that you are strong and determined. You can accomplish the things you aspire to do, whether that involves new skills, tools, education, or even a new lifestyle. I'm sure as a child that you read, *The Little Engine That Could.* The engine, facing a seemingly impossible hill, starts to talk to itself: *I think I can, I think I can.* Believing its own words, the engine pulls the train up that hill. That's who we are— accomplished and Ambitious Women who, at times, like the little engine, have learned to replace any doubts with the phrase, "I think I can, I think I can," which soon becomes, "I know I can, I know I can."

Remember when I talked about the importance of our "self-talk"? Well, our self-talk will retrain our minds to believe the words, "I know I can, I know I can." Our self- talk helps us to interpret our feelings and experiences. In a sense it's a gauge that allows us to evaluate thoughts and actions and make decisions about responding to our world.

Our self-talk is the internal conversation we have with ourselves that determines our perceptions and beliefs. When we become like the Little Engine, our self-talk will bring about positive feelings that become positive actions.

Touching Lives

We want to succeed for ourselves, and we want to reach out to others. The more we do this, the more we fulfill ourselves. We gain every time we touch the life of someone else; we enrich our own and enhance theirs. As women, part of our identity is the connection we achieve with others. We fully understand this. We've learned that the more we give, the more we receive. We reach out not because we have to; we reach out because it is a part of us that seeks to be given recognition.

The author and poet Maya Angelou said, "I've learned that people will forget what you said, people will forget what you did, but people will never forget how you made them feel." When we experience the joy of touching others, we become a part of their lives forever. Think of those people who have touched your life. You may no longer be in contact, but you still remember the hand they offered. That's the reason we give of ourselves: not for pride, and not for gain. We give to others because we've experienced what it is like to receive; we recognize the value in it, and we genuinely care about those with whom we connect. Sharing who we are, and our gifts and talents, helps us continue to be whole and healthy. Clearly, reaching out to others is an integral part of what makes us unique. This life journey upon which we've embarked, with the goal of reaching beyond ourselves, includes a variety of elements.

"Nothing changes if nothing changes." This statement, which has been paraphrased by many, sums up our decisions and choices. As Ambitious Women, we already know this—if we don't seek and grasp change, there will be no change. Yet consider how much more powerful we are when we make those decisions to change—when our attitude is future-thinking and not past-seeking.

We are our most powerful agents of change, and we have discovered how true this is as we've read through the chapters of this book. We've had the opportunity to look at others who demonstrate the concepts we value, and we gain both knowledge and excitement from them.

In many ways, it's as if we see ourselves as the pioneer women we learned about in school. They left the comforts of home and community to settle the West with few supplies, but with enormous vision and dreams. We need to recognize that same determination in ourselves and face forward as we continue on our life journey. This is exciting, this is our future, and this is how we see ourselves. This is the image we present to others in our lives; and as Ambitious Women, we are not afraid to grow and change and to take charge of our own futures.

One of the characteristics of our growth and change is how we learn and practice accountability. We do this by affirming who we are, upholding the dignity and integrity of ourselves and others, and reaching out. We can advocate for ourselves, family, and friends, and for co-workers and neighbors. As we put ourselves in the position of being an advocate, we affect the lives of those around us. This is more than the common view of working on behalf of someone who is hospitalized; it is a way we can choose to direct our lives. We are accountable and recognize our responsibility for our thoughts, actions, and words.

WHEN WE ARE GENUINE, WE ARE REAL. We don't wear the masks that may have protected us in the past because we've learned to be free of the expectations of others. We've let ourselves out of the box of "expected" and "predictable." We are genuine and authentic in our feelings, behavior, and words. We present ourselves openly and honestly; we know who we are.

Life Goals

Setting goals is an integral part of our continued growth; it means we never just settle, that we're keeping our faces forward. When we focus on a goal—whether it is learning how to make perfect pasta, prune rose bushes, or increase our technology skills—we are identifying a direction in which we choose to travel. Our goals are specific; some are short-term while others are more long- range. They give us a map of where we're headed, and how we choose to get there. As we set goals, we find natural ways to overcome any hesitation we may have. A goal is concrete and has an end result. It is tangible: a representation of who we are and where we are headed.

We are powerful and we never give up. We reach out with encouragement and help, and we give encouragement and help to ourselves as well. We are coaches and/or mentors to those around us. In these capacities, we touch the lives of our children, family members, friends, and strangers alike. We have mentors, coaches, and accountability partners to help in our quest for success. We never arrive.

As Ambitious Women, we involve ourselves in relationships in which we explore dreams and hopes and determine which actions and strategies will help others and ourselves blossom. This is a transformational relationship; our intent is to connect with others and ourselves and offer encouragement and enthusiasm.

Powerful Words

There are those people who have touched us, and we have benefited and grown from their impact on our lives. And we do the same—we offer ourselves to others, we pour into them, and they receive benefits just as we did.

As Ambitious Women, we offer hope to others— hope that whatever is desired is possible, that no one is alone in their journey. When we hope, we commit with our hearts and believe anything is possible; we can and do grow and thrive in any circumstance. When we reach out to another, when we offer hope in our smile, our gestures, and our words, we are reaching into the future.

Ambitious Women are women who are always willing to learn from the women who have gone before us. One important thing we do is to NEVER SETTLE. We are always looking forward, reaching out, and learning and growing with enthusiasm. The more we do this for ourselves, the more it becomes a natural, automatic part of who we are. As such, it rubs off us and affects those around us. We are willing to learn in every aspect of our lives—in our work, personal, family, social, and church worlds—and doing so enhances us and aids us as we stretch and grow.

> "Do one thing every day that scares you."
>
> **—Eleanor Roosevelt, former First Lady**

I encourage you to ponder and reflect on Mrs. Roosevelt's statement; it encourages us to not shy away just because something is unfamiliar or different. Instead, we are to reach outside of ourselves and do one thing that is different every day. This is a way we can challenge ourselves and aim higher and farther. There is no need to settle back and not strive; that is not a part of who we are at this point in our journey.

I have two final messages that I want to share with you. One is the encouragement to be true to who you are, to decide to no longer seek approval; instead, trust who you are and how you are doing at any given moment. Always affirm yourself, especially when no one else will. Remember, there is ONLY ONE YOU. No one else was created like you, and no one else can do what you can do. Believe this: The world is a better place with you in it.

The other message is the importance of our desire to reach out to others, to not live in a void. We share who we are, and we encourage others. We bless others as we reach out to them from the fullness of ourselves. As we bless others, we help them to recognize their own value. Perhaps this is the greatest gift we can give—pouring from ourselves into others.

When we reach out to others, we are, indeed, spreading light. This is unselfish and a way in which we make our impact on our world. As Ambitious Women, we receive great joy from this; we love helping, sharing, encouraging, and blessing others. Fortunately, there is no end point; we NEVER ARRIVE because we are always seeking, learning, and growing. It is an exhilarating process, and one we can enjoy throughout our lives!

I'm not saying we should not be content. Contentment—meaning we are at peace with ourselves and where we are in life—helps us to truly be happy in life. However, contentment doesn't mean we "just settle" or that we are fully satisfied. To say that you are satisfied can be the same as giving up on your dreams, your goals. And if you ever feel *completely* satisfied, you may not have set your goals high enough. Don't settle for mediocrity. Go from being good to being great!

Accept the fact that life won't always be smooth sailing. You will certainly have days when you will not be at your best, and that's okay. But don't stay there. And don't let others tell you that you aren't good enough or that you will never amount to anything. You are not average because average means you have "arrived." Instead, never stop believing in yourself or think something you want to do or change in your life is out of your reach—it is not! Just keep striving to improve, to better yourself, to move one step closer to your goal.

Are you the person you want to be?

Have you done the things in life you truly want to do? You should always be growing, always be reaching, always be improving.

Now go out and live life to the fullest every day! YOU ARE AN AMBITIOUS WOMAN!

Chapter 19

10 Characteristics of Ambitious Women

Live Your Life On Purpose

Most all of us have dreams, ambitions, goals or aspirations … at least of some kind. Things we want to do or become.

But sometimes life can get in the way. We may have the best of intentions but the day-to-day, the responsibilities, and the busyness can leave us merely trying to survive, much less thrive. Days turn into weeks, and weeks turn into years, and if we aren't careful, we can find ourselves living but not being truly alive.

The good news though is that it doesn't have to be this way.

As Ambitious Women, we can do ANYTHING if we make the choice to do so.

We can have a clear picture of who we are, who we want to become, what we are created for in this life. The "who we are" was answered in the pages of this book. They are the sum total of an Ambitious Woman. As we endeavor to add these character traits, we will become the "who you want to be." Yet to truly feel fulfilled, we need to understand what we are created for.

Notice I didn't say "what we want to do." Why? Because whenever we think of what we want to do, we get lost in a maze of ideas and we lose focus in the confusion. Then we say, "I don't know what I want to do." But when we find out what we were created to do, what we want to do comes easily.

Here are some specific points for you to consider and contemplate in order to live your life on purpose.

1. **Believe.** As an Ambitious Woman, you have a dream or an idea you want to pursue. But unless YOU believe in it, unless YOU believe you are capable of fulfilling your goals, you will never bring your dream into reality. Remember, what you dream of and how you want to live your life on purpose is part of your core being. As a Christian person I believe your dreams and ideas are God's gift to you. Consider this quote from the Bible: "For I know the plans I have for you," declares the Lord, "plans to prosper you and not to harm you, plans to give you hope and a future." Wow, God has plans for you, and he has put them inside of you! That doesn't mean your road to success will be a bed of roses. Nothing good in life ever comes about without hard work, persistence, and determination. The resistance is part of our journey in life and is what helps us to grow, making our success that much sweeter.

2. **Perfection is Unachievable**. If you wait until you are perfect, if you wait until you have your dream perfectly in your heart, you will never move forward. The truth

is that perfection is unachievable unless you are God … and I'm sure if you have looked in the mirror lately, you know that you are not him. Waiting for things to be perfect, for you to be perfect, is just an excuse not to begin your journey to success. Every successful person I know is a doer. Yes, they think things through but they don't overthink it to the point of inaction. At some point you must do or you'll just keep wishing you did.

3. **Keep the Big Picture in Mind**. Whatever you want to achieve, realize that you are in a marathon, not a sprint. There is almost no such thing as an "overnight success." People who have achieved success, who have lived out their dreams, have done so through hard work and years of step-by-step moving forward. When you keep the big picture in mind, you will be intentional about what you are doing. And being intentional will keep you on the path you are meant to travel in order to achieve your success.

4. **Check Your Motivation**. Sadly, our society sets us up to fail. There is always someone better looking, more successful, someone who has achieved more, done more. Our society focuses on the external, like wealth, fame, and beauty. If you chase after these, it is like chasing after the wind. You can see them, feel them, sense them, but they will always slip through your grasp. Instead of going after the external, focus on your personal growth, on developing healthy relationships, and seeing a win-win in everything you do.

5. **Live with Integrity**. One of the greatest company mission statements I have heard was stated by Jere Thompson, Jr.: "Never Sacrifice Integrity for Growth." Do you know what you stand for? Do you strive to do the right thing, even when no one is looking? Do you live by your values? Are your values consistent in your everyday life? Are you at peace with yourself? If you can answer "yes" to these questions, then you are an Ambitious Woman who lives with integrity. But if you answered "no" to even one of these questions, then I can guarantee you that you do not feel fulfilled. So print these questions out and ask yourself each one as you get ready for the day and before you go to bed.

6. **Step Out**. Too many people live within their comfort zones. They say they are happy. They may even be successful. But are they fulfilled? Being fulfilled involves stepping out of the known into the unknown. To truly live life on purpose, you should never settle for what is comfortable. Whatever your dream is, whatever goal you wish to achieve, will, by its very nature, make you feel uncomfortable. Don't shy away from the discomfort; embrace it. Make it part of who you are. Then use it as "fuel" to move you down the road you have always wanted to travel.

7. **Be a Hero**. Within every movie, every fiction book, and every great novel there is something called the "hero's journey." Your hero's journey is your core being crying out to you. It is the unique path in life that only you can take. It is what you were made to do. It can be

scary to be a hero … and it can be the most fulfilling thing you will ever do. In Mariah Carey's song "Hero" she sings about looking inside of yourself and staying strong, because eventually you'll find a hero in you. As an Ambitious Woman, I challenge you to follow your hero's journey through to the end of your life.

8. **Stay Focused**. We all have strengths. And we all have weaknesses. Yet, there is something about human nature that makes us focus on our weaknesses at the cost of using our strengths. I recommend that you spend 75% of your time and energy developing your strengths—your character and your talents—and 25% on your weaknesses. Yes, it is good to overcome a weakness so that it becomes a strength. But if you can reach the point where your weaknesses are minimized and no longer hurt you, then your sense of fulfillment will skyrocket.

9. **You Don't Need Approval.** When we first entered the world, people loved us. They made us feel special. In fact, most of us received our validation from those around us. But as we grew into adulthood, fewer and fewer people were there to offer us this same validation. So we go about our lives trying to be what others want us to be, who they say we should be, and do what they say we should do. We wear masks that fool us into thinking we are living a fulfilled life. But the more we listen to others and do what they tell us to do, the less we are living life on purpose. Here is a truth: you cannot live someone else's vision of **who you are**. YOU HAVE TO BE YOU! As an Ambitious Wom-

an, you can choose to be indifferent to what people think of you, to what they want—even demand— you to be. I did not say that you "blow them off." But you don't need the validation of others to accomplish what you want to do. Just be yourself. In fact, give yourself permission to be yourself. When you do, you won't be nearly as worried about what others say about you. Do you recall the oldie-but- goodie song by Sammy Davis Jr., "I've Gotta Be Me"? He sings that he can't be anyone but himself. And that's the way we all should be. The less you look for other people's approval, the more of it they'll give to you.

10. **Live Life on Purpose**. Follow your dreams. Achieve your goals. Don't be afraid to step out. As an Ambitious Woman, you can decide today that you are no longer going to settle for the average, the norm, the mundane day-to-day. You can decide today that you are no longer going to live a boring, unfulfilled life. If you make this decision today, when you look back on this moment in a few weeks, months, and years, you will see that it was a defining moment in your life—the moment you decided to live life on purpose!

The moment you decided to be THE AMBITIOUS WOMAN

About the Author

Born Esther Kerene Lahr in Amarillo, Texas, Esther was raised in Southern California. As an adult, she began her professional career by becoming the first female order desk clerk for General Electric/Hotpoint in Los Angeles. In her 20s, she moved to San Diego and met the love of her life, Frank Spina, at a church volleyball game, Singles vs. Marrieds. Five months later, they eloped to Yuma, Arizona, and together they started life by building a successful ceramic tile construction business and raising four children. When the recession of the 90s hit California, they moved to the Fort Worth area of Texas where Esther became an independent sales rep for a national company. She became part of a Top Producing District and Regional Office and achieved the Senior Representative position, as well as being a Top Producer for that company ten years in a row.

In 2006, Esther became a marketing consultant, and within three years she was promoted to National Consultant, the highest level in the company. Her passionate work ethic and distinguished sales strategies helped her to earn numerous accolades including Top-10 money earner ten years in a row and Millionaire Club member 7 years in a row. Esther was personally selected by the CEO of the company to receive the elite leadership award, for her invaluable combination of leadership, integrity, teamwork, and character.

In 2008, Esther concentrated her passion of developing others personally and professionally by founding a network called Ambitious Women. Since then, she and a group of like-minded women have hosted ten annual conferences focused on building and developing the businesses and lives of women.

Esther also takes great pride in her personal developments, specifically her family. Esther and Frank, have four grown children, Aaron, David, Peter, and Rachel, and 7 beautiful grandchildren, Katherine, Luke, Samson, Owen, Esther, Hannah and Joshua—and still counting! Working diligently to earn a financially free lifestyle is a cornerstone to Esther's success, and she wants to help others realize that same success as well.

Contact Information

Esther Spina www.estherspina.com
http://ambitiouswomenconference.com/

Ambitious Women Show

www.directsales.tv

Contact info: esther@estherspina.com

www.Facebook.com/estherspinaambitiouswoman
www.Twitter.com/SpinaEsther

www.Instagram.com/Esther_Spina
www.Linkedin.com/in/EstherSpina

CPSIA information can be obtained
at www.ICGtesting.com
Printed in the USA
BVHW040811230321
603242BV00012B/1270

9 781628 655223